D0956551

CULTURE SMART!
ISRAEL

Jeffrey Geri

·K·U·P·E·R·A·R·D·

First published in Great Britain 2007
by Kuperard, an imprint of Bravo Ltd
59 Hutton Grove, London N12 8DS
Tel: +44 (0) 20 8446 2440 Fax: +44 (0) 20 8446 2441
www.culturesmartguides.com
Inquiries: sales@kuperard.co.uk

Culture Smart! is a registered trademark of Bravo Ltd

Distributed in the United States and Canada
by Random House Distribution Services
1745 Broadway, New York, NY 10019
Tel: +1 (212) 572-2844 Fax: +1 (212) 572-4961
Inquiries: csorders@randomhouse.com

Copyright © 2007 Kuperard

All rights reserved. No part of this publication may be reprinted or
reproduced, stored in a retrieval system, or transmitted in any form or
by any means without prior permission in writing from the Publishers.

Series Editor Geoffrey Chesler
Design Bobby Birchall

ISBN 978 1 85733 344 2

British Library Cataloguing in Publication Data
A CIP catalogue entry for this book is available from the
British Library

Printed in Malaysia

This book is available for special discounts for bulk purchases for
sales promotions or premiums. Special editions, including
personalized covers, excerpts of existing books, and corporate
imprints, can be created in large quantities for special needs.

For more information in the U.S.A. write to Special
Markets/Premium Sales, 1745 Broadway, MD 6–2, New York,
NY 10019 or e-mail specialmarkets@randomhouse.com.

In the United Kingdom contact Kuperard publishers at the
address at the top of the page.

Cover image: View of Tel Aviv from Jaffa. *Travel Ink/David Forman*
The picture on page 89 is reproduced by permission of Hila and Eitan Rubin-Razinsky.
The images on pages 13, 19, 49, 65, 118, 127, 129, 132, 137, 139, and 142 are reproduced
by permission of the Israel Ministry of Tourism.

CultureSmart!Consulting and **Culture Smart!** guides have both
contributed to and featured regularly in the weekly travel program
"Fast Track" on BBC World TV.

About the Author

JEFFREY GERI is a South African-born writer living in Tel Aviv. After graduating with a B.Com LLb from the University of Witwatersrand, he practiced as a barrister before leaving *Apartheid* South Africa in the early 1960s to make his home in Israel. He has been involved in all aspects of Israeli life. He has brought up three Israeli sons and worked extensively in tourism and advertising. He has written several novels, two of which, *Oh Henry* and *The Trouble With Francis*, are based on the theme of immigration to Israel, and travel articles for the Israeli English-language press.

Other Books in the Series

Other titles are in preparation. For more information, contact: info@kuperard.co.uk

The publishers would like to thank **CultureSmart!**Consulting for its help in researching and developing the concept for this series.

CultureSmart!Consulting creates tailor-made seminars and consultancy programs to meet a wide range of corporate, public-sector, and individual needs. Whether delivering courses on multicultural team building in the U.S.A., preparing Chinese engineers for a posting in Europe, training call-center staff in India, or raising the awareness of police forces to the needs of diverse ethnic communities, we provide essential, practical, and powerful skills worldwide to an increasingly international workforce.

For details, visit www.culturesmartconsulting.com

contents

contents

Map of Israel

LEBANON

• Kiryat Shmona

GOLAN HEIGHTS

SYRIA

Nahariya •
Acre (Akko) •
Rosh Pina •
Safed •
SEA OF GALILEE (KINNERET)
Haifa •
Karmi'el •
Tiberias •
MOUNT CARMEL

MEDITERRANEAN SEA

Nazareth •
• Afula

Caesarea ▲

Hadera •

Netanya •

WEST BANK

Herzliya •
Tel Aviv-Jaffa •
• Petach Tikvah

JORDAN

Ashdod •
Rehovot •
• Ramle

Ashkelon •

Jerusalem •

DEAD SEA

GAZA

Masada ▲

Beersheba •

Dimona •

JORDAN

NEGEV DESERT

EGYPT

Eilat

GULF OF AQABA

introduction

Culture Smart! Israel sets out to condense an extremely complex subject into a compact guide that will help you discover the Israel behind the clichés. This dynamic, diverse, and paradoxical country is steeped in history and biblical associations, yet most Israelis are modern, secular, and energetically materialistic. Visitors from abroad will find much that is familiar, and more that is unexpected. To soften the impact of the latter, this book offers insights and essential human information that will deepen your understanding of the Israeli people and enable you to make the most of your visit.

Israel embraces its many visitors—tourists, businesspeople, foreign representatives, pilgrims, and, most of all, those who have come to stay. The Israelis love showing off their country and its not inconsiderable accomplishments over less than sixty years of statehood. They glow when a returning guest says, "I can't believe the development that I have seen," or when a business traveler says, "Next time I'll bring my family," and they are genuinely upset when it happens, as is inevitable with over two million tourists a year, that the occasional visitor has a bad experience. Israelis like to be liked.

So, for now, *Bon Voyage* through these pages. You will read about the formative influence of Israel's ancient and modern history, its geography, and what makes Israelis the way they are. You will acquaint yourself with Israel's democratic institutions, rich cultural life, wide range of cuisines, sports and leisure opportunities, sandy beaches, and lively city streets, and you will understand its dilemmas.

The Israelis you will meet will be from all walks of life. They will be more or less sophisticated depending on their occupations, where they live, or where they were brought up. They will almost always be friendly, helpful, and direct—perhaps to a fault—and resourceful. Some will be well mannered; others won't. A few may be Holocaust survivors; many will be the children of Holocaust survivors. They will all carry with them memories of Israel's wars, in which relatives, comrades, and loved ones fell in defense of the country.

Finally, you will learn what to expect and how to behave in different social circumstances, so that you can make genuine friends and valued business partners. Israelis are great travelers, and those whom you visit may one day visit you.

"*Bruchim Habaim*!" Welcome!

Key Facts

Official Name	The State of Israel	(Hebrew, *Medinat Israel*)
Capital City	Jerusalem	Population approx. 750,000
Main Cities	Tel Aviv (pop. 1.2 million), Haifa (pop. 450,00), Beersheba (pop. 200,000) Other cities: Netanya, Eilat, Nazareth, Tiberias, Ashdod, Petach Tikva	
Population	6,900,000	5.26 million Jewish; 1.35 million Arabs (mostly Muslim); 0.29 million others
Area	1967 borders: 8,019 square miles (20,770 sq. km)	Slightly smaller than both New Jersey and Wales
Location	Eastern Mediterranean, between Gaza and Lebanon	
Terrain	Varied: coastal plain; hilly northern and eastern regions; Jordan Valley; Negev desert in south	
Coastline	170 miles (278 km)	
Climate	Mediterranean temperate. Hot and dry in the southern and eastern deserts. Rain in winter. The coastal plain is humid, the hilly interior and Galilee are cooler.	

Language	Modern Hebrew, spoken with a Sephardi pronunciation. Written in the Hebrew alphabet from right to left.	Second official language: Arabic Many other languages are spoken, with English predominating.
Religion	Judaism	
Minority Religions	Islam, Christianity, Druze, Baha'i	
Government	Parliamentary democracy with a single-chamber parliament, the Knesset	The head of state is the president. The head of government is the prime minister. There is an independent judiciary.
Currency	New Israeli shekel (NIS) (100 agorot = 1 NIS)	
Media	There are four Hebrew TV channels plus satellite and cable TV. Many different radio stations	Four Hebrew daily newspapers and eleven other language dailies, including two in English. International publications are widely available.
Electricity	220 volts (50 Hz)	3-pronged angled plugs are used.
DVD/Video	PAL system	
Telephone	Israel's country code is 972, followed by the area code and number	To dial out of Israel, dial 00 or 013, 012, or 014.
Time Zone	GMT + 2 (summer time). GMT + 1 (winter time)	

chapter one

LAND &
PEOPLE

GEOGRAPHY

Situated at the eastern end of the Mediterranean
Sea, Israel is a narrow strip of land bordered to the
north by Lebanon; to the east by Syria, the West
Bank, and Jordan; to the south by the Red Sea; and
to the southwest by Egypt. A new border, added by
Israel's recent disengagement, is that of the Gaza
Strip, a slim finger of land pointing along the coast
from the Sinai Peninsula, ending just south of the
Israeli city of Ashkelon.

Israel has been compared in size to the state of
New Jersey and to the country of Wales, but with a
climate and topography that varies greatly from north
to south and from east to west. Along the
Mediterranean on the verdant coastal plain are two of
its three main cities: Tel Aviv–Jaffa, "the city that never
sleeps," and, about 53 miles (85 km) north, Haifa,
serene and beautiful on the slopes and crest of Mount
Carmel. Haifa is the port city gateway to the Galilee,
with its landscape of hills, forests, and olive groves
and, at its lowest point, below sea level, the Sea of
Galilee. There are no mountains in Israel, only hills.

Jerusalem, Israel's spiritual capital and seat of government, nestles in the biblical Judean hills 37 miles (59 km) east of Tel Aviv. East of Jerusalem is the Judean desert, which slopes down to the Dead Sea, the lowest point on earth, and the start of the Great Rift Valley that runs south through Africa to Mozambique.

About 71 miles (115 km) south of Tel Aviv lies Beersheba, the capital of the Negev Desert, and a 150-mile (241 km) journey further south through the desert, to its southernmost point, takes you to the Red Sea port and resort of Eilat.

CLIMATE

Israel enjoys a Mediterranean climate with hot, rain-free summers and mild winters, which have intermittent periods of heavy rain, particularly in the north and center of the country. From April to October daily temperatures range from 73.4°F (23°C) low to 86°F (30°C) high, with July and August the hottest months. From November to March temperatures range from 59°F (15°C) low to 68°F (20°C) high. In the winter, from the northern

Galilee to the northern Negev, the country is transformed into a deep green. You are unlikely to encounter snow, but if you do it will be in winter in Jerusalem or on the Golan Heights. Temperatures and tempers rise during the occasional *Hamsin* (*Sharav* in Hebrew), a hot, dry, desert wind occurring mostly in early summer and fall.

Jerusalem is cooler than the coastal plain, especially in the evenings, and enjoys lower humidity. Eilat is always warmer, and is a winter sunshine favorite for Israelis and foreign visitors alike, as are the Dead Sea resorts.

A BRIEF HISTORY

The State of Israel was established in 1948, in a land holy to three of the world's great religions— Judaism, Christianity, and Islam. Unsurprisingly, interpretations of its history are hotly contested, but to understand the Israelis one must start with the Jewish perspective.

Ancient History

Jewish history began about 4,000 years ago (c. 1600 BCE) with the biblical patriarchs Abraham, Isaac, and Jacob. The Book of Genesis relates how Abraham, a native of the Sumerian city of Ur, in today's southern Iraq, was commanded to go to Canaan to found a community that worshiped the

One God. When a famine spread through Canaan, Abraham's grandson Jacob (Israel), his twelve sons, and their families moved to Egypt, where their descendants were forced into slavery.

Modern scholarship is continually refining our understanding of the historical context of the biblical account, but the powerful narrative of the Hebrew Bible is the foundation stone of Jewish identity. Thus, after generations of bondage in Egypt, Moses led the Israelites to freedom, to receive the revelation of the Ten Commandments at Sinai, and to be forged into a nation by forty years of wandering in the desert. Joshua spearheaded the conquest of Canaan, the promised land of milk and honey, where the Children of Israel were bound to establish a moral and ethical society that would be "a light unto the Gentiles." The exodus from Egypt, indelibly implanted in Jewish consciousness, is still celebrated by Jews every year, wherever they may be, at *Pesah* (Passover), the festival of freedom.

The Biblical Kingdoms of Israel (c. 1000–587 BCE)
The Israelites settled in the central hill country of Canaan more than a thousand years before the birth of Christ. These were the years of the biblical Judges, Prophets, and Kings. The hero-king David vanquished the Philistine champion

Goliath, and his kingdom, with Jerusalem as its capital, became a power in the area; his son Solomon built the first Temple in Jerusalem in the tenth century BCE. He made political alliances through marriage, expanded foreign trade, and promoted domestic prosperity. After his death the kingdom was split into two: the kingdom of Israel in the north with its capital at Shechem (Samaria), and the kingdom of Judah in the south with its capital at Jerusalem.

Exile and Return

The small Jewish kingdoms were caught up in the power struggles of the day, between the rival empires of Egypt and Assyria. In about 720 BCE, the Assyrians destroyed the northern kingdom of Israel and dispatched its inhabitants into oblivion; in 587 BCE the Babylonians destroyed Solomon's Temple and transported all but the poorest Jews to Babylon. Throughout the period of exile the Jewish people retained their faith: "If I forget thee O Jerusalem, let my right hand forget its cunning" (Psalm 137.5). After the Persian conquest of Babylon in 539 BCE, Cyrus the Great allowed the exiles to return and rebuild the Temple. Many Jews remained in Babylon, and communities grew up in every major city around the Mediterranean. Thus began the pattern of coexistence of a Jewish presence in the land of Israel with Jewish communities in the outside world, known collectively as the Diaspora (dispersal).

In 332 BCE Alexander the Great conquered the region. After his death in 323 BCE his empire was divided up, with Judah eventually falling to the Syrian portion ruled by the Seleucid dynasty. Their Hellenizing policies were resisted, and they were expelled in an insurgency led by the priest Mattathias and his son Judah Maccabee, who rededicated the defiled Temple in 164 BCE, a victory celebrated to this day in the festival of Hanukkah. The Jewish royal house they founded, the Hasmoneans, ruled until Pompey's siege of Jerusalem in 63 BCE, after which the Jewish state was absorbed into the Roman Empire.

Roman Rule and the Jewish Revolts

In 37 BCE Herod, son of an Idumaean chieftain, was appointed King of Judea by the Roman Senate. Granted almost unlimited autonomy in the country's internal affairs, he became one of the most powerful client kings in the eastern part of the Roman Empire. Herod kept his subjects ruthlessly in check, and launched a massive construction program, which included the cities of Caesarea and

Sebaste, and the fortresses at Herodium and Masada. He also rebuilt the Temple in Jerusalem, making it one of the most magnificent buildings of its time. Despite his many achievements he failed to win the trust and support of his Jewish subjects.

Herod's death in 4 CE was followed by years of political turmoil, civil unrest, and messianic fervor. Cruel and corrupt Roman procurators united the disparate Jewish factions against them, and in 67 CE the Jews rose up in a general revolt. The Emperor Nero sent his general Vespasian to Judea with three legions. After Nero's suicide in

68 CE, Vespasian ascended the imperial throne, and sent his son Titus to continue the campaign in Judea. In 70 CE the Roman armies laid siege to Jerusalem, and on the ninth day of the Hebrew month of Av the Temple was burned to the ground. All other buildings, except for three towers, were razed, and the city's population was taken captive.

A band of Zealots had taken refuge at Masada, the fortress palace built by Herod on a barely accessible mountain plateau overlooking the Dead Sea. In 73 CE, after years of trying to dislodge them, the Romans besieged the fortress with an army of ten thousand men. When they eventually succeeded in breaching its defenses, they found that all but five of the defenders, men, women and children, had committed suicide rather than face crucifixion or enslavement.

A second, better-coordinated Jewish revolt broke out in 131, under the spiritual leadership of Rabbi Akiba and the generalship of Simon Bar Kochba. The Romans were forced to evacuate Jerusalem, and a Jewish administration was set up. After four years, and very heavy Roman losses, the revolt was put down by the Emperor Hadrian in 135 CE. Jerusalem was rebuilt as a Roman city dedicated to Jupiter, Aelia Capitolina, and Jews were forbidden to enter it. Judea was renamed Syria Palaestina.

The Diaspora

The story of the dispersal of the Jews outside the land of Israel is long and complex, and the subject of a great body of literature. Ironically, the destruction of the Temple cult gave rise to a vigorous new form of religious and social cohesion—rabbinical Judaism, the system of law and custom that was heir to the scholastic tradition of the Pharisees.

From 135 CE onward, for almost two millennia, the Jews lived as a distinctive minority among other nations. As Israel's first Prime Minister, David Ben Gurion, put it, "We have preserved the Book, and the Book has preserved us." In the Christian world Jews were subjected to nearly constant persecution. They fared better under Islam—the "Golden Age" in Muslim Spain was a high point in Jewish history. Elsewhere, in different times and places, there were periods of peace, prosperity, and cultural achievement. The land of Israel, in the meantime, was coveted and fought over by a succession of rulers, each with his own agenda.

Byzantine Rule (327–637)

After the destruction of the Jewish state, and with the adoption of Christianity as the official religion of the Roman Empire, the country became predominantly Christian and a center of Christian pilgrimage. Queen Helena, the Emperor Constantine's mother, visited the Holy Land in 326; churches were built in Jerusalem, Bethlehem, and Galilee, and monasteries founded throughout the country. A Persian invasion in 614 caused havoc, but the Byzantines retook the country in 629.

The First Muslim Period (638–1099)

The first Muslim occupation began four years after the death of the Prophet Mohammed, and lasted more than four centuries. In 637 Jerusalem was taken by Caliph Omar, who was unusually tolerant toward Christians and Jews alike. In 688 the Umayyad Caliph Abd el-Malik, based in Damascus, commissioned the magnificent Dome of the Rock on the site of the Temple on Mount Moriah, from where the Prophet Mohammed was carried on his famous night journey. The al-Aqsa mosque was built close to the Dome. In 750 Palestine passed to the Abbasid caliphate and was governed from their new capital, Baghdad. In 969 it fell to the Shi'ite Egyptian Fatimids (known to the Europeans as Saracens); the Church of the Holy Sepulcher was destroyed, and Christians and Jews were harshly suppressed.

The Crusaders (1099–1291)

Christians had generally worshiped freely in Jerusalem under Muslim rule. In 1071, however, the nomadic Seljuk Turks, newly converted to Islam, defeated the Byzantine Emperor at Manzikert near Lake Van, and expelled the Fatimids from Palestine and Syria. In 1077 they closed Jerusalem to Christian pilgrims. The Byzantine Emperor and pilgrims appealed to Pope Urban II for help in 1095. In response he called for a Crusade, or holy war, to liberate the Holy Land from the heathen. Between 1096 and 1204 there were four major European Christian campaigns to the Middle East.

In July 1099, after a five-week siege, a great Crusader army led by Godfrey de Bouillon captured Jerusalem, massacring most of the city's non-Christian inhabitants, and burning its synagogues with the Jews inside. Godfrey established the Latin Kingdom of Jerusalem. On his death in 1100 he was succeeded by his brother, Baldwin. From the mid twelfth century, however, the Christian territories were on the defensive, despite the formation of the great military-religious orders of the Knights of St. John and the Knights Templar.

In 1171 the Seljuks of Mosul destroyed Fatimid power in Egypt and installed their Kurdish general Saladin as ruler there. The impact was electrifying. Saladin swept through Galilee and defeated the Christian army under Guy de Lusignan at the Horns of Hattin near Lake Tiberias, before taking Jerusalem in 1187. In the region, only Tyre, Tripoli, and Antioch remained in Christian hands. In response the Europeans mounted the Third Crusade. Under the leadership of Richard the Lion-Heart of England, the Crusaders managed to recapture a narrow strip of the coast, including Acre, but not Jerusalem. Richard returned to Europe after making a truce with Saladin. Later campaigns by European monarchs, including the future Edward I of England, came to nothing. Finally, the Mameluke Sultanate of Egypt reconquered Palestine and Syria, taking the last Christian outpost in 1302.

Mameluke Rule (1291–1516)

The Mameluke dynasty, descended from Turkish and Circassian slave soldiers, held power in Egypt from 1250 to 1517. Under their rule Palestine entered a period of decline. Ports were destroyed to prevent further crusades, and commerce dwindled. Ultimately the country, including Jerusalem, was virtually abandoned; the small Jewish community was totally impoverished. In the final period of Mameluke rule the country was beset by power struggles and natural disasters.

Ottoman Rule (1517–1917)

In 1517 Palestine became part of the expanding Ottoman Empire, as part of the *vilayet* (province) of Damascus-Syria. The present walls of Jerusalem were built by Suleiman the Magnificent in 1542.

After 1660 it became part of the *vilayet* of Saida (in Lebanon). At the commencement of Ottoman rule, there were about 1,000 Jewish families living in the country, descendants of Jews who had always lived there as

well as immigrants from other parts of the Ottoman Empire. In 1700 work started on the "Hurva" synagogue in the Old City of Jerusalem. In 1831 Mohammed Ali, the Egyptian viceroy nominally subject to the Sultan of Turkey, occupied the country and opened it up to European influence. Although the Ottomans reasserted direct control in 1840, Western influence continued. In 1856 the Sultan issued the Edict of Toleration for all religions in the empire, and Jewish and Christian activity in the Holy Land increased.

The desire to return to the land of Israel (Hebrew, *Eretz Yisrael*) had been preserved in the liturgy and folk consciousness of the Jews since the time of the destruction of the Temple in 70 CE. Belief in the return of the Jews to Zion was part of Jewish messianism. Thus, long before the invention of political Zionism, Jewish attachment to the Holy Land found expression in *Aliyah* ("ascension," or immigration) to *Eretz Yisrael*. Supported by Jewish philanthropy, Jews came from countries as far flung as Morocco, Yemen, Bukhara, Romania, and Russia. In 1860 Jews established the first settlement outside Jerusalem's city walls. Before Zionist colonization began there were already sizeable Jewish communities in Safed, Tiberias, Jerusalem, Jericho, and Hebron. The Jewish population in the country as a whole grew by 104 percent between 1890 and 1914.

Zionism

Zionism was the name adopted in 1890 by the Jewish national movement that sought to establish an independent Jewish homeland in Palestine. The word "Zion" referred at first to the hill in Jerusalem on which King David built the Temple. In time it became synonymous with the Temple, the city, and the Holy Land itself.

In eighteenth-century Europe, the Enlightenment had seemed to herald an age of tolerance and reason in which Jews could participate as equals in civic society. But emancipation brought new problems as assimilated Western Jews entered the middle classes and the professions. Secular European nationalism spawned both modern "scientific" racist and mystical-nationalist forms of anti-Semitism.

In underdeveloped Tsarist Russia the officially inspired pogroms of the 1880s—the pillage, rape, and murder of the Jews in their unprotected rural settlements—strengthened the feeling that Jewish salvation lay in an independent homeland and gave urgency to the ancient religious longing for a return to Zion. Initially without any coherent plan, the Zionist movement under Theodore Herzl developed a political program to obtain sovereign rights in Eretz Yisrael.

THEODORE HERZL

An assimilated Austrian-Jewish intellectual, Herzl was the Paris correspondent for the *Neue Freie Presse* of Vienna, an influential liberal newspaper, during the notorious Dreyfus Affair. He reported on and was shaken by the outbreak of mass anti-Semitism in France over the court martial in 1894 of Alfred Dreyfus, a French Jewish army officer convicted of spying for Germany on the basis of forged evidence.

The Dreyfus trial convinced Herzl that in an age of nationalism the only solution to the Jewish predicament was political—the creation of a Jewish state. With energy and determination he dedicated himself to the cause, writing a pamphlet entitled *Der Judenstaat* (*The Jewish State*) in 1895. He canvassed the support of influential Jews and ideologically disparate Zionist groups, and convened the first Zionist Congress in Basel in 1897. In all, between 1897 and 1902 he convened six Zionist Congresses, creating the infrastructure and the tools for a concerted political effort.

Herzl's 1902 novel *Altneuland* ("Old-New Land"), setting out his vision of a cooperative Jewish commonwealth in Palestine, reflects many of the prevailing nineteenth-century ideas of progressive and socialist utopias. His opening words were, "If you will it, it is no dream."

Herzl met with world leaders and government ministers in an effort to obtain stopgap sites to locate the Jewish State, and to elicit their encouragement and support. Alternative sites proposed were Palestine, Cyprus, the Sinai Peninsula, and El Arish. The British Colonial Secretary Joseph Chamberlain's offer in 1903 of East Africa (Uganda) was unacceptable, particularly to the Russian Congress delegates.

Long recognized as the leader of modern Zionism, Herzl died in 1904. He was buried in Vienna, and after the establishment of the State his remains were brought to Israel and reburied on Mount Herzl in Jerusalem.

The Balfour Declaration

The effort to secure a Jewish homeland won a measure of support with the Balfour Declaration of 1917, which declared Britain to be in favor of the establishment of a national home in Palestine for the Jewish people.

At the same time, in the course of the First World War, undertakings were given to Arab national leaders to encourage them to rise up against their Ottoman masters. After the War, the Ottoman Empire was dismembered; and the newly founded League of Nations granted Great Britain a mandate to govern Palestine on both sides of the Jordan River.

The British Mandate (1919–48)

The terms of the Palestine Mandate incorporated Article 6 of the Balfour Declaration, undertaking to facilitate and encourage Jewish immigration and settlement while ensuring that the rights and positions of other sections of the population were not prejudiced. It was also based upon the principle that the mandated territory be brought to independence as soon as possible. Thus,

having made contradictory promises, Britain was embarking on a near-impossible mission. One of its first acts, in 1922, was to create the Emirate of Trans-Jordan on the east side of the Jordan River. Jews were permitted to settle only in western Palestine.

Immigration
Between 1919 and 1939 successive waves of Jewish immigrants arrived in Palestine, contributing to the growth and development of the local Jewish community, or *Yishuv*. About 35,000, mainly from

Russia, came between 1919 and 1923. They laid the foundations of an advanced social and economic infrastructure, returning to the land and establishing unique communal and cooperative forms of rural settlement—the *kibbutz* and the *moshav*.

The next influx of some 60,000, between 1924 and 1932, arriving in the main from Poland, was drawn to the cities and contributed to the expansion of urban life. They settled mainly in the new city of Tel Aviv, in Haifa, and in Jerusalem, where they set up small businesses, construction firms, and light industry. The last major wave of immigration took place in the

1930s, following Hitler's rise to power in Germany. The newcomers, some 165,000, many of whom were professionals and intellectuals, constituted the first large-scale immigration from Western and Central Europe and had a considerable impact on the community's commercial and cultural future.

Palestinian Arab opposition to Zionism expressed itself in riots and massacres in the 1920s—in Hebron, Jerusalem, Safed, Haifa, Motza, and elsewhere—and a general Arab revolt in 1936–8, led by Haj Amin Al-Husseni (and financed by the Axis powers), in which Arab and Jewish paramilitary groups clashed for the first time. Britain responded to the situation with the Peel Commission in 1937, which recommended partition into Jewish and Arab states, with British control of Jerusalem and Haifa, which the Jews reluctantly accepted but the Arabs rejected.

War with Germany was now looming, and Britain, anxious to secure Arab support throughout the region, redefined its Palestine policy in the MacDonald White Paper of 1939. This effectively put an end to further Jewish immigration, and prohibited the purchase of land by Jews—denying the Jews of Europe refuge in Palestine and abandoning them to their fate. Ships carrying Jewish refugees were turned back. Some sailed around the world in search of refuge in other countries, some were sunk. The White Paper caused a shocked *Yishuv* to reevaluate its relationship with Britain, and led to a more militant Zionist policy.

The Jewish Underground

Three Jewish underground movements operated during the British Mandate period. The largest was the Haganah, founded in 1920 by the Zionist Labor movement to safeguard the security of the Jewish community. It responded to restrictions on Jewish immigration with mass demonstrations and sabotage. The Etzel, or Irgun, established by the opposition nationalist Revisionist movement in 1931 (and later led by Menachem Begin, who became Israeli Prime Minister in 1977), carried out covert military actions against both Arab and British targets. The smallest and most extreme group, the Lehi, or Stern Gang, started terrorist activities in 1940. The three movements were disbanded with the establishment of the State in 1948.

Palestine's Jewish Volunteers in the Second World War

With the outbreak of the Second World War, the *Yishuv* concentrated on helping Britain in the fight against Germany. Over 26,000 men and women of the Jewish community in Palestine served in the British forces in the army, air force, and navy. In

September 1944, the Jewish
Brigade was formed as an
independent military unit of
the British army, with its own
flag and emblem, comprising
some 5,000 men. The Brigade
saw action in Egypt, northern

Italy, and northwest Europe. After the Allied
victory in Europe, many Brigade members
contributed to the clandestine effort to bring
Holocaust survivors to Palestine.

The Holocaust

It is not possible to disentangle the conflict in the
Middle East from the Nazi Holocaust. Nothing in
all the years of dispersal could have prepared the
Jewish people, or the world, for the horror of their
fate during the Second World War. In a systematic
plan, on an industrial scale, the Nazi regime set
out to liquidate the Jews of Europe, murdering six
and a half million, including one and a half
million children. As the German armies
conquered one European country after another,
Jews were rounded up and herded into ghettos.
From the ghettos they were transported to
concentration camps where they died of disease
and starvation, were shot in mass executions, or
put to death in gas chambers. The few who
escaped the dragnet fled to other countries, joined

the partisans, or were hidden by non-Jews at risk of their own lives. Only one-third of European Jewry, including those who had left Europe before the war, survived. Not until the end of the war did the world learn of the magnitude of the genocide and the depths to which humanity had sunk. For most Jews, whatever their previous positions, the establishment of a Jewish homeland and sanctuary was now a humanitarian necessity, a moral imperative, and an expression of the Jewish determination to survive.

After the Second World War

After the war, Britain increased the restrictions on the number of Jews permitted to enter and settle in Palestine. The *Yishuv* responded by engaging in "illegal immigration," organizing a network of activists to rescue Holocaust survivors. Between 1945 and 1948, some 85,000 Jews were smuggled into the country by secret, often dangerous, routes, in spite of a British naval blockade and border patrols. Those who were caught were interned in detention camps on Cyprus or returned to Europe.

Jewish resistance to the Mandate increased, and the different Jewish underground groups contributed to an escalating cycle of violence culminating, in 1946, in a bomb attack on the British military headquarters in the King David

Hotel in Jerusalem, in which ninety-one people were killed. Amid mounting tension Britain handed the problem of Palestine over to the United Nations. Lobbying continued, and a special UN committee visited Palestine and made its recommendations.

On November 29, 1947, with U.S. and Soviet support, despite bitter opposition by the Palestinian Arabs and neighboring Arab states, the United Nations voted to partition Palestine into two: a state for the Jews and a state for the Arabs. The Zionists accepted this; the Arabs rejected it. Riots broke out in Palestine and across the Arab world. In January 1948, while Britain was still nominally in control, an Arab "Army of Liberation," organized by the Arab League, arrived in Palestine to join the local Palestinian paramilitary organizations and militia. They invited the world's media to observe specially staged maneuvers.

Britain declared its intention to withdraw in May, and refused to hand over authority to any body—Arab, Jewish, or United Nations. In the spring of 1948 the Arab forces blocked the Jerusalem–Tel Aviv road, cutting off Jerusalem from the rest of the Jewish population.

The War of Independence
On the day the British finally withdrew, May 14, 1948, the State of Israel, with 650,000 Jewish

inhabitants, was formally proclaimed, with Chaim Weizmann as its President and David Ben Gurion as Prime Minister. The Declaration of Independence read, "The State of Israel will be open to the immigration of Jews from all the countries of their dispersion."

The following day, Israel was attacked by the armies of Egypt, Jordan, Syria, Lebanon, and Iraq. This was a fight for survival. In the course of the conflict thousands of Palestinian Arabs fled to the

neighboring Arab countries, where, in the absence of a peace treaty, they remained refugees. By the ceasefire of January 7, 1949, the Israelis had driven the Arab armies back, and had added substantially to the territory allocated to them in the UN resolution. Afterward most of the area designated by the UN as an Arab state, including East Jerusalem and the Old City, was annexed by Jordan.

After 1948 Israel doubled its population in four years through immigration. The displaced Jews of Europe were now joined by some 600,000 Jews fleeing persecution in Arab lands. The successful absorption of so many newcomers from totally different cultures into the fabric of a tiny host community, while that community was still sorting out its basic infrastructure, is without precedent and a huge achievement.

KEY EVENTS SINCE 1948

The years since the establishment of the State have been turbulent and dramatic, with far-reaching consequences for the wider region. Paradoxically, the implacable hostility of its neighbors has helped bind Israeli society together and been a stimulus to growth and invention.

1956: The Sinai Campaign

In 1955 Egyptian president Gamal Abd al-Nasser blockaded the Gulf of Aqaba, cutting off the port of Eilat, and established a unified command with Jordan and Syria. In July 1956 he nationalized the Suez Canal, and closed it to Israeli shipping. In October, Israeli forces, in a preemptive strike, took control of the Sinai Peninsula. Under intense U.S. and UN pressure, Israel withdrew after receiving international assurances that her vital waterways would remain open.

1960: The Eichmann Trial

Adolf Eichmann, chief administrator of Hitler's extermination program, was kidnapped in Argentina by Israeli intelligence agents and brought to Israel to stand trial. Found guilty of crimes against humanity and the Jewish people, he was sentenced to death and hanged on May 30, 1962. This is the only sentence of capital punishment given in the history of the State of Israel.

1967: The Six-Day War

Nasser massed troops in the Sinai Peninsula, expelled the UN observer force from the border with Israel, and closed the Red Sea Straits of Tiran to Israeli shipping. King Hussein of Jordan placed his army under Egyptian command and admitted Iraqi forces into the country. In Israel, General Moshe Dayan was appointed Minister of Defense. Yitzhak Rabin was the Chief of Staff.

On June 5, in a surprise predawn raid, Israeli planes destroyed the Egyptian air force on the ground. Ground forces moved into Sinai and, in a repetition of the 1956 Sinai Campaign, sped toward the Suez Canal. After Jordanian and Syrian attacks, Israel captured East Jerusalem, the Jordanian West Bank, and the Syrian fortifications on the Golan Heights. In six days the war was over. The Gaza strip and entire Sinai Peninsula, the Golan Heights, including the southern slopes of Mount Hermon, and the West Bank up to the Jordan River, including the Old City of Jerusalem, were in Israeli hands.

1972: Munich Olympic Games Massacre

At the 1972 Olympic Games in Munich eleven Israeli athletes were taken hostage by Palestinian terrorists, and then killed by their captors during a botched rescue attempt by the German security forces.

1973: The Yom Kippur War

Egypt and Syria launched coordinated attacks on Yom Kippur, the holiest day in the Jewish year—a day of fasting, when the streets are clear of traffic and neither radio nor television are on the air. Arab gains at the outset were substantial. Two weeks later the situation was reversed, albeit with heavy losses. Israeli forces under General Ariel Sharon had crossed the Suez Canal and surrounded the Egyptian Third Army.

1976: Entebbe

An Air France plane on the way to Tel Aviv was hijacked by Palestinian terrorists and flown to Entebbe, Uganda. In a bold and dramatic mission, Israeli troops flew out to Africa and rescued the passengers who were being held hostage at Entebbe Airport.

1977: Menachem Begin Prime Minister

For the first time since the establishment of the state, the Likud Party, under the leadership of Menachem Begin, defeated the Labor Party in elections and formed a right-wing government.

1979: Peace With Egypt

In 1979, two years after Egyptian President Anwar Sadat's historic address to the Knesset in Jerusalem, and a year after signing the Camp David Accords under the auspices of U.S. President Jimmy Carter, Israel and Egypt signed a formal peace treaty in Washington. This was the first peace treaty with an Arab country.

1981: Bombing of the Iraqi Nuclear Reactor

In June 1981, Israeli planes bombed Iraq's Osirak nuclear reactor, removing the immediate threat of Saddam Hussein's nuclear weapons program.

1982: Invasion of Lebanon

In response to attacks on Israel's northern towns and villages by the Palestine Liberation Organization, led by Yasser Arafat, Israeli forces entered southern Lebanon. Initially intending to advance no further than forty kilometers, they swept on to Beirut. The PLO fighters were shipped out ignominiously to Tunisia, but world opinion, and facts on the ground—including the infamous massacre of Palestinians in the Sabra and Shatila refugee camps by the Lebanese Christian Phalangists—forced Israel to withdraw to a narrow strip north of its border.

1987: The First Intifada

In the West Bank and Gaza Palestinians demonstrated violently against the Israeli occupation. A campaign of commercial strikes, rallies, and stone-throwing disrupted life in Israel and the territories.

1991: The Gulf War

After the American-led coalition's invasion of Iraq in January–February 1991, Saddam Hussein launched Scud ballistic missiles against Israel. Fortunately these did not have chemical warheads and missed almost all their targets.

1993: The Oslo Accords

Secret talks in Oslo between Israeli and Palestinian negotiating teams resulted in an agreement under which there would be mutual recognition and a cessation of violence. Its signing, on September 13, 1993, was preceded by an exchange of letters between PLO Chairman Yasser Arafat and Prime Minister Rabin, in which the PLO renounced the use of terrorism, pledged to invalidate those articles in its Covenant that denied Israel's right to exist, and committed itself to a peaceful resolution of the decades-long conflict. In response Israel recognized the

PLO as the representative of the Palestinian people. Palestinians in the West Bank and Gaza Strip would, step by step, become self-governing, and Israel would halt settlement activities in the territories.

1994: Peace with Jordan

Following the Oslo Peace Accords with the PLO, Israel signed a formal peace treaty with Jordan.

1995: The Oslo Interim Agreement

This broadened Palestinian self-government through an elected self-governing authority, the Palestinian Legislative Council (elected in January 1996), and the continued redeployment of the Israel Defense Force in the West Bank. It also set out a procedure that would lead to a Final Status Agreement.

1995: The Assassination of Prime Minister Yitzhak Rabin

On November 4, 1995, Israel's Prime Minister, Yitzhak Rabin, was shot and killed by a right-wing Jewish fanatic at a peace rally in Tel Aviv.

1996: A series of suicide bombings on buses and elsewhere carried out by members of the Islamic fundamentalist terror group Hamas undermined the peace process and the government of Shimon Peres.

1996: The right-wing Likud leader Benjamin Netanyahu was elected prime minister.

1998: The Wye River Plantation talks resulted in agreement on Israeli redeployment and release of poltical prisoners, and renewed Palestinian commitment to the Oslo principles.

1999: The Labor leader, former general Ehud Barak, was elected prime minister in a landslide victory on a peace platform.

2000: In May, Israeli troops were withdrawn completely from southern Lebanon.

2000: Camp David Talks

In July, U.S. President Clinton, Prime Minister Barak, and Palestinian Chairman Yasser Arafat met at Camp David to hammer out a final settlement. The negotiations came tantalizingly close to an agreement, but ended in failure.

2000: The Second Intifada (the al-Aqsa Intifada)

Palestinian riots broke out after opposition leader Ariel Sharon visited the Temple Mount on September 28, although his visit had been officially announced and approved in advance with Palestinian officials, including Arafat himself. This second, more lethal, Intifada was characterized by suicide bombings in buses, markets, shopping malls, and places of entertainment in Israel, and, in the territories, by car shoot-outs and knifings. Stringent antiterrorism measures were instituted.

2001: Ariel Sharon was elected prime minister in a landslide victory over Labor, promising "peace and security."

2002: In response to a large number of suicide bombings, Israel started operation "Defensive Wall" in the West Bank, arresting Palestinian leaders and blockading Yasser Arafat in his headquarters in Ramallah.

2003: The "Roadmap"

On May 25, 2003, Israel accepted the "Roadmap," a peace plan devised by the U.S., the UN, the E.U., and Russia. This sought a two-state solution to the Israeli-Palestinian conflict, to be reached in three stages.

From the Israeli perspective, the Palestinians have failed to live up to their obligations under the first phase of the Roadmap (unconditional cessation of terrorism and an end to incitement). Among the measures taken by Israel against terrorism has been the construction of an anti-terrorist barrier—part wall, part fence—around the West Bank.

2003: The Aqaba Summit

In June the new Palestinian prime minister Mahmoud Abbas and Ariel Sharon called for an end to violence and pledged to abide by the Roadmap. The rejectionist movements Hamas and Islamic Jihad vowed to continue the violence.

2003: On November 19 the UN Security Council passed Resolution 1515 in support of the Roadmap for peace.

2004: On November 11 Yasser Arafat, Chairman of the PLO, died.

2005: In January Mahmoud Abbas was elected President of the Palestinian National Authority.

2005: Sharm El Sheikh Summit Conference

In February Prime Minister Sharon, President Abbas, President Mubarak of Egypt, and King Abdullah of Jordan met in Egypt to restore peace. The Intifada was declared over.

Within weeks a suicide bomb exploded in Tel Aviv. Israel froze a planned handover of Palestinian towns. Following another suicide bomb in Netanya, Israel responded with a massive anti-terror manhunt. Hamas launched rocket attacks from Gaza.

2005: Disengagement from Gaza

In August Sharon, former champion of the settler movement, unilaterally pulled Israeli forces out of the Gaza Strip, evacuating 8,000 settlers and dismantling twenty-one settlements plus another isolated four in the West Bank.

2006: Middle East Shakeup

Sharon caused an earthquake in Israeli politics when he left Likud to form a new centrist party, Kadima. He then suffered a massive stroke that left him in a coma with little chance of recovery. His deputy, Ehud Olmert, took over the reins of government and led the party to victory in the 2006 general elections.

The Palestinian Authority elections of 2006, too, produced a shock result. To its own surprise, Hamas, the Islamist organization whose declared aim is the destruction of Israel, won a landslide majority, defeating the incumbent Fatah party. Many interpreted this victory as a vote for better governance rather than for continued conflict.

In June 2006, the kidnapping of an Israeli soldier within Israel by Hamas infiltrators from Gaza provoked a renewal of hostilities in the south. A few weeks later, Hezbollah, the Iranian-backed Shi'ite militia in southern Lebanon, rocketed Israel and kidnapped two Israeli soldiers in a cross-border raid. Israel responded with massive airstrikes followed by a ground invasion. Hezbollah launched thousands of rockets into Israel and engaged the IDF in guerrilla warfare. A month later the UN Security Council passed Resolution 1701, which called for a cessation of hostilities and "the disarmament of all armed groups in Lebanon, so that . . . there will be no weapons or authority in Lebanon other than that of the Lebanese state," and strengthened the role of the UN Interim Force on the border. At the time of writing the situation is still unfolding.

ISRAELIS TODAY

If first-time visitors expect to find Israelis, as a whole, much like their Jewish acquaintances, friends, or business associates back home, they are in for a surprise. The Israeli nation is made up of ethnically and culturally diverse types, reflecting the populations of their counties of origin. Thus, Israelis whose parents came from the Yemen look like Yemenites, slight with dark complexions, and those from Iraq look like Iraqis. Many Russian immigrants resemble the very Cossacks who carried out pogroms in the late nineteenth and early twentieth centuries.

Between 1948 and 1977 waves of Jews (about 745,000 in all) arrived in Israel from Muslim countries where their situation was becoming untenable. After the North African immigration in the 1950s came Poles, Dutch, "Anglo-Saxons" from the U.S.A. and the British Commonwealth, French, South Americans, Mexicans, Greeks, Turks, and other nationalities—a huge mosaic, not only of physical types but of cultures, values, and customs. Their Israeli-born children and grandchildren are called "Sabras," after the fruit of the desert cactus plant—thorny on the outside and sweet on the inside. They carry on the traditions of their parents, or, in the case of intermarriage, might combine the two.

Russians and Ethiopians

In the 1990s, Israel successfully absorbed more than a million immigrants from Russia and the former member states of the Soviet Union. This massive influx made a large impact on the country, substantially increasing not only the population, but also the available pool of skills and talent in technology, science, art, music, dance, and physical education. A negative impact was the growth of organized crime.

In 1984 around 7,000 Ethiopian Jews were brought to Israel in "Operation Moses." In 1991 they were joined by another 14,500, rescued in "Operation Solomon" in thirty hours, just before the fall of Addis Ababa to the rebel Ethiopian People's Revolutionary Democratic Front. Differences in culture, background, tradition, and expectations made it more difficult for these new immigrants to integrate as a community, but there have been many individual success stories, particularly in fashion and the military.

Israel is also home to a widely diverse non-Jewish population. Of its present population of 6.9 million people, approximately 77 percent are Jewish, 19 percent are Arab, and the remainder consists of Druze, Circassians, and others.

Israeli Arabs

Israeli Arabs, whose forebears did not flee the conflict in 1948, are citizens, voters, and office holders. They are well represented in Parliament, either through their own parties or as members of the mainstream political parties, are members of trade unions, and many are enrolled in Israel's universities. Israeli Arabs live harmoniously alongside their Jewish fellow citizens in Haifa, Acre, Jaffa, and Ramle. They run their own towns and villages through democratically elected town councils, and practice in all the free professions.

On the negative side, Israel's Arabs are trapped in the middle of the Middle East conflict, which not only creates divided loyalties, but also undoubtedly affects the attitudes of many Jewish Israelis toward them, arousing mutual feelings of suspicion and distrust. Israeli Arabs are not required to serve in the Israeli Army.

There are Israeli Arab success stories in every sphere: political, cultural, media, entertainment, and sports, to name a few. Some examples are the soccer players Ababas Suan and Wallid Badir, who are members of the 2006 Israeli national team. There is a Jewish–Arab Youth Orchestra, which recently performed under the baton of Daniel Barenboim. Amal (meaning "hope") Muricus, a beautiful young Israeli Arab woman, is a popular singer with a large following, and in 1999, beauty queen Rana Raslan became the first Arab "Miss Israel."

The Bedouin

Less constrained by notions of nationality, the Bedouin are a nomadic people who mainly live in the southern Negev. Their tents, camels, goats, and sheep can be seen from the main roads. They have a reputation for generous hospitality, and a meal in a Bedouin tent is a memorable experience for the guest. They are renowned for their tracking prowess, and many serve in the IDF as volunteer trackers guarding Israel's borders.

Rumor has it that some Bedouin, in addition to herding and tracking, are also heavily involved in smuggling.

The Druze

This closely knit community is an Ismaili sect that originated in eleventh-century Cairo around the cult of the Fatimid Caliph al-Hakim. They have succeeded in keeping their religion a total secret, known only to their priests and initiates.

Those Israeli Druze who live in villages scattered throughout the Galilee have been successfully integrated into Israeli society. They serve in the IDF, where many attain high rank, and are for the most part free from the dilemmas faced by Israeli Arabs. On the other hand, the Druze living in the villages on the Golan Heights do not know whether or not the Golan will be returned to Syria, and thus have a problem deciding where their allegiance lies. The Golan Druze are not drafted into the IDF.

The Circassians

Muslims but not Arabs—they originated in Circassia (Cherkessia in Russian), a region in the Caucasus near the Black Sea—they are concentrated in villages in the Lower Galilee. They look Eastern European, and in addition to Hebrew speak their own language, Circassian, and Arabic. They are regarded as Israeli in all respects.

GOVERNMENT

Israel is a democratic republic based on universal suffrage. Its key institutions are the presidency, a unicameral parliament (the Knesset), the government, the judiciary, and the State Comptroller.

The President

Although his duties are largely ceremonial, the president is the Head of State and his office symbolizes the unity of the nation above and beyond party politics. A parliamentary majority elects the president for one term of seven years.

Parliament (the Knesset)

The main function of parliament is to legislate. General elections, based on a system of proportional representation, determine its composition, and 120 members operate through plenary sessions, twelve standing committees, and three special committees. Parliament  is elected for a tenure of four years but may be dissolved earlier by itself or by the prime minister.

The Government (Cabinet)

The government is the executive arm of the state with responsibility for administering internal and external affairs, including security, and, although accountable to Parliament, it is equipped with wide-ranging powers.

The government is formed after an election when the president presents the party leader mostly likely to succeed with a mandate to submit a list of cabinet ministers for the approval of Parliament. The list must be presented together with proposals of policy within twenty days. Once approved, the ministers become responsible to their leader, the prime minister, and to Parliament. Most cabinet members receive a portfolio: defense, foreign affairs, etc. Others serve without a portfolio.

The Judiciary

Judges are appointed by the president on recommendations made by a special nominations committee consisting of Supreme Court judges, members of the bar, and public figures; they are appointed for life with mandatory retirement at the age of seventy. Civil and criminal cases are heard in magistrates' and district courts, while juvenile, traffic, military, labor, and municipal matters are dealt with in their own special courts. There is no trial by jury in Israel. In matters of personal status such as marriage, divorce, and adoption, jurisdiction is vested in the courts of the religious institutions of Israel's various communities.

The Supreme Court is the highest court of appeal, which can overturn the rulings of lesser tribunals. It hears petitions against any government body, in which case it is the court of first and last instance. It can also make recommendations to Parliament regarding the desirability of legislative modifications, and has the authority to respond to petitions, to determine whether the implementation or interpretation of a law conforms with the intention of Israel's basic law. Israel has no written constitution; however, most of the chapters of what would comprise a constitution are already there in the form of basic laws, including "Human dignity and liberty (1992)."

The State Comptroller
The State Comptroller, elected by Parliament for a seven-year term of office, carries out an internal audit and reports on the legality, regularity, effectiveness, and moral integrity of the public administration, and is authorized to inspect the financial affairs of the parties represented in Parliament. He has no power to implement his findings, and although his reports are widely publicized in the media, not enough is done to ensure that his findings are acted on.

Elections

Parliamentary elections are general, national, direct, equal, and secret, with the entire country being one electoral constituency. Voters cast one ballot for the political party they wish to represent them in parliament. The large number of parties competing for election reflects a wide range of philosophies and beliefs concerning religious, social, security, and economic issues.

Prior to the election, each party presents its platform and list of candidates, and parliamentary seats are assigned in proportion to the number of votes the party receives as a percentage of the national vote. Since the establishment of the state,

ten to fifteen parties have been elected to every parliament, and no single party has ever obtained a majority. The result has been one coalition after another, with inherent instability, backstabbing, and the wielding of undue influence by marginal parties, especially the religious parties.

The two main political parties, traditionally one left and one right, are now both moving to the center. The smaller parties may be characterized as national religious, ultra orthodox, liberal left wing, nationalist right wing, and Arab parties. Minorities are represented in all Israeli parties.

Every citizen is eligible to vote from the age of eighteen and to be elected to parliament from the age of twenty-one.

Israelis take a great interest in politics, both in internal and security affairs and in foreign relations. Although there is traditionally a high electoral turnout, 77 to 87 percent of eligible voters, in the 2006 election that brought the new centrist party, Kadima, to power, and in the election that preceded it, voter turnout was only a little more than 60 percent.

According to one of the Basic Laws (laws dealing with constitutional issues) the Knesset, through the Central Elections Committee, may prevent a party from participating in elections if its objectives or actions, expressly or by implication, include denial of the legitimacy of the State of Israel as the state of the Jewish people; denial of the democratic character of the State; or incitement to racism.

Election Day

Election Day is a public holiday so that everyone can vote. Soldiers on active duty vote in polling stations in their units. Special arrangements are made for prison inmates to vote, as well as for those confined to hospital.

Israeli law does not provide for absentee ballots, and voting takes place only on Israeli soil.

The sole exceptions are Israeli citizens serving on Israeli ships and in Israeli embassies and consulates abroad.

The government is installed when the Knesset has expressed confidence in it by a majority of 61 Knesset members, and the ministers thereupon assume office.

THE ECONOMY

Despite a dearth of natural resources, Israel has developed into a modern industrial state with a technologically advanced economy. Imports are primarily crude oil, grains, raw materials, rough diamonds, and military equipment. Leading exports are cut diamonds, high-technology products (Israel today is a world leader in high tech), industrial and agricultural products, chemicals, fashion, and security services. Israel's military and software industries include high-tech products for aviation, communication, medical electronics, and fiber optics. Four Israelis are on the Forbes One Hundred list.

Israel suffers from a negative import/export balance but has a positive balance of payments due to large unilateral transfers and outside loans. Roughly half of its outside debt is to the U.S.A., its major source of economic and military aid. In 2004 the real growth rate was 3.9 percent. The labor force was an estimated 2.68 million, with an unemployment rate estimated at 10.7 percent.

THE ISRAEL DEFENSE FORCE (IDF)

The Israel Defense Force's mission statement is to defend the existence, territorial integrity, and sovereignty of the State of Israel; to protect the citizens of Israel; and to combat all forces of terrorism that threaten daily life.

The IDF is a citizens' army and the draft is a significant factor in Israeli life. With few exceptions all Israeli men and women are required to serve in the army, for three years in the case of men and two years in the case of women. After completion of military service a man is obliged to carry out military reserve duty for a number of weeks every year, depending on the needs of the unit to which he belongs, until the age of forty-one. Above the age of twenty-four women are not required to do reserve duty, apart from those with special skills. Women are barred from active combat but make excellent instructors, and young male conscripts learn weaponry, marksmanship, and other skills from them.

Young Israelis from different backgrounds, origins, economic circumstances, and levels of education do their basic training and complete their military service together, and year after year meet up again in reserve duty (*miluim*), irrespective of what they do in daily life. Strong bonds are forged. The IDF is a unique social mechanism that helps to integrate new immigrants and transform them into Israelis.

The units young people serve in and their achievements are testimonials that accompany them throughout their lives, like prestigious public schools or major universities in other countries.

In its official Web site, the IDF sets outs the basic points of its doctrine as follows:

The IDF's defensive strategy is to rely on a small standing army with an early warning capability, a regular air force and navy, and an efficient mobilization and transportation system.

Its offensive tactics are the use of multiarm coordination, quickly transferring the battle to the enemy's territory, and finally the quick attainment of war objectives.

The IDF sees itself as an army with a civilized ethos, based on its military heritage and the traditions of the State of Israel—its democratic principles, laws and institutions, the traditions of the Jewish people throughout their history, and, most importantly, moral values that affirm the value and dignity of human life.

The IDF trains its servicemen and women to set a personal example in carrying out their duties, to be conscious at all times of the value of human life, and to use their weapons sparingly so as not to harm noncombatants. It requires its servicemen and women to carry out their duties with professionalism and discipline, to refrain from giving or carrying out illegal orders, and to demonstrate true comradeship and a conscious sense of mission in defending the state of Israel.

The IDF is always ready to render assistance to the victims of revolutions, wars, and major natural disasters, and over the past years has participated in many international rescue and support missions in countries such as Mexico, Georgia, Rwanda, Turkey, Kosovo, and Kenya.

CITIES AND TOWNS

Israel's three main cities, Jerusalem, Tel Aviv, and Haifa, differ substantially from each other. It is said that Tel Aviv dances, Jerusalem reflects, and Haifa stands in beauty. These cities are discussed below. Other main towns include the major Red Sea resort of Eilat; Beersheba, capital of the Negev; Ashkelon, an industrial, residential, and resort town with a good beach, holiday clubs, and marina; Ashdod, Israel's second-largest port, given a boost by its high percentage of new Russian immigrants; and Netanya, a busy residential, commercial, and resort town with splendid beaches and a fine promenade. Other interesting towns are described in Chapter 7.

Jerusalem

High up in the Judean hills, Jerusalem, the capital of Israel, is steeped in three thousand years of history. With a metropolitan population of 750,000, it is the seat of government, the Knesset (parliament), the Supreme Court, and the judiciary. A short distance away from these institutions is the Old City, whose holy sites, for Christians, Muslims, and Jews, are religious and sacred landmarks.

Tel Aviv

Tel Aviv, in English "the Hill of Spring," has a metropolitan population of 1.2 million. Variously called "the first Hebrew city in the modern state of Israel," "the White City," "the city that never sleeps," and the "biggest little city in the world," Tel Aviv–Jaffa hugs nearly nine miles (fourteen kilometers) of Mediterranean coastline.

"The first Hebrew city" was founded in 1909 when a group of Jewish residents of the ancient port city of Jaffa moved out of their overcrowded and hostile surroundings and established their own community north of Jaffa's borders.

The Seashell Lottery

Legend has it that a "seashell lottery" was held on the beach to arrange a fair distribution of land among the sixty families who bought it. The names of the families were written on sixty white shells and the numbers of the plots on sixty gray shells, and the pairs of gray and white determined the distribution.

The city expanded greatly, neighborhood by neighborhood, during the years 1934 to 1939 with the huge influx of European immigrants escaping from Hitler, most of whom were educated and cultured, and who imparted a character and personality to Tel Aviv that has endured ever since. They created a sophisticated "Mittel Europa" on the sand dunes under the blue skies of the eastern Mediterranean.

Nearly a quarter of Israel's Jewish population lives in the Tel Aviv metropolitan area. There is little division between the financial, commercial, and residential districts, so few areas shut down after office hours. Sister cities include Ramat Gan, a famous diamond center; Bat Yam, known for its

beaches; Rehovot, for the world-renowned
Weizmann Institute of Science; Herzliya, for its
beaches, marina, and high technology; and Bnei
Brak, for prayer and religion.

Haifa

The northern coastal city of Haifa has a
metropolitan population of 450,000. Populated
since biblical times, and associated with the
prophet Elijah, it came to life with the building of
the Haifa–Damascus railway in 1905. Jewish
immigration at the end of the First World War
and the harbor built by the British during the
years 1929 to 1934 gave the city a major boost.

Haifa is Israel's most important port and naval
base, and provides port facilities for the American
Sixth Fleet. The country's main industrial center,
it is the site of Israel's oil refineries, and produces
a wide range of products including electronic
equipment, chemicals, glass, steel, and cement.
Unlike Jerusalem, which is divided into three—
west for Jews, east for Arabs, and the Old City for
all—Haifa is a city in which Jews and Arabs live
together harmoniously. It is also the world center
of the Baha'i faith.

Haifa has an underground funicular railway,
the Carmelite. Stenciled at the end of each car is
Leviticus 19:32, "Stand for an elderly person." It is
the only city in Israel where public transportation

runs on Saturdays, the Sabbath, which says much about the city.

THE KIBBUTZ

The political theorist and philosopher A. D. Gordon (1856–1922) believed that physical work would create a link between the settlers and their new land, and would prevent them from exploiting it like old-fashioned colonialists. With this in mind, in 1910 a group of twelve Russian idealists established Degania, the first communal settlement, or *kibbutz*, at the southern end of the

Sea of Galilee. Fired by a vision of a new Socialist era, they believed that what they were doing would be imitated throughout the world. Others followed, and a wave of settlements of the same kind spread all over the *Yishuv*.

In fact, the communal structure of the kibbutz owed more to the pressing need to solve problems than to socialist ideology. The inhospitable terrain of rocky hills, marshes, and mosquito-breeding swamps had to be cleared. In order to achieve this, and to deal with disease and protect themselves from unfriendly neighbors, they pooled their resources and relied upon each other, in the process creating a closed community where security needs, labor, and its rewards were equally shared. An elected committee decided on strategy and priorities, allocated tasks, and organized the provision of basic needs.

"Kibbutzniks" have made a contribution to the state out of all proportion to their numbers, reaching influential positions in politics and high ranks in the army, where many are prominent in elite volunteer units.

Today there are around three hundred *kibbutzim* in Israel, with a population of roughly 100,000. Some kibbutzim are religious; some have well-run and attractive guesthouses, particularly those in the scenic locations.

Many kibbutzim have established factories, often as joint ventures with outside companies, and this has had an eroding effect on kibbutz life, gradually replacing absolute equality with the infrastructure necessary to compete profitably, including salary differentials, and the employment of outside labor and people with special skills. Some of these factories have been very successful. About twenty-five kibbutz industries have so far gone public.

Another factor contributing to the erosion of their original values is that many kibbutzim permit and even encourage members to work outside the kibbutz framework. Some of these people earn high salaries, and after contributing a basic sum to the kibbutz are allowed to keep the balance. Many receive company cars and other corporate perks. Some kibbutz members also have outside sources of income derived from gifts or inheritances. There is even a plan for members to own their homes.

Many kibbutzim accept volunteers, mostly young European backpackers, who spend weeks or months living and working on the kibbutz.

THE MOSHAV

Apart from the kibbutz, there have been many other forms of settlement in the country, both agricultural and urban. The *moshav* is a looser arrangement than the kibbutz. It is a farmers' cooperative in which families farm their own land, live in their own houses, and lead independent lives, but conduct marketing and the acquisition of agricultural equipment collectively. Some members rent out their land while they work in the cities. Others have used their land to establish agriculture-related industries.

chapter two

VALUES &
ATTITUDES

WARS AND OCCUPATION

The fight for survival has made, and continues
to make, a profound impact on the Israeli
psyche. With one exception (the prosecution of
the 1982 war in Lebanon) there has always been
consensus among Israelis about the threat to
their country's existence and the fate in store for
them should they lower their guard.

This is not so with regard to the Occupation.
Over the years, the right-wing's vision of a
"greater Israel" has been eroded, and today
views range from those of a small minority of
extreme right-wingers, who still cling to their
maximalist dream, through those of the vast
majority, who would like, with the exception of
East Jerusalem and the Old City, to end the
Occupation and retain only those areas vital to
Israel's security, to a small left-wing minority
who would like to return to the 1967 borders
with minor changes.

RELIGION

Israel's Jewish population is generally thought of as consisting of two groups, religious and secular, with the latter dominant. In fact, Israeli Jews are divided into four groups. The smallest group, the black-hatted, black-coated ultra-Orthodox, according to a survey conducted in 1995, amounts to about 8 percent of the total. They are not conscripted into the army, and support their own political parties, differing from each other, to the outside eye, more in form than in substance. The religious parties in Parliament wield considerable power because their general lack of interest in the larger picture makes them potentially flexible coalition partners. Money is basically what they are interested in, to fund their schools, charities, and community welfare projects, and if they get it they are satisfied.

Two other groups combine to form the religious Zionists, whose male members almost universally wear knitted skullcaps (*kippot*), and who observe, to the letter, the tenets and traditions of the Jewish religion as laid down in the Scriptures and interpreted by their rabbis.

According to the same survey, they comprise about 17 percent of the population. They serve in the army, many attaining high rank, and are identified with the right wing in the political arena. Most of the settlers recently evacuated from Gaza belong to this group.

The third group, the largest at about 55 percent of the total, is made up of the so-called "traditionalists." They observe those practices that

suit their lifestyle, and make their children aware of their traditions, but oppose a formal reformation of the Jewish religion, believing it to be unnecessary and negative. At the back of their minds is the thought, perhaps, that an intact Judaism kept its adherents going for more than two thousand years, and question whether a watered-down version would do as well. Where's the harm in leaving it the way it is?

And finally there are the secular, who are perhaps not as secular as they claim to be. Looking at the survey, religious or traditional Jewish practice intrudes quite substantially on secular Israeli life. Almost every Jewish male is circumcised, and almost without exception every

Jewish home has a *mezuzah* (a little parchment scroll of prayer in a case) affixed to the doorpost of the house. Fewer than 20 percent of thirteen-year-old Jewish Israeli boys do not celebrate *bar mitzvah*, fewer than 20 percent do not have Jewish wedding ceremonies and burials, and 95 percent always or sometimes participate in the annual Passover celebration. Some secular Jews actually fast on the Day of Atonement (*Yom Kippur*) and almost a third, sometimes or always, observe the dietary laws of *Kashrut* in their homes. The secular claim that these anomalies arise out of family values rather than belief. Perhaps, but more than 87 percent of Israeli Jews believe that there is a God, and roughly the same number think it may be true that the Ten Commandants were given to Moses on Mount Sinai—all of which has nothing to do with family values. These statistics emerge from a survey by the prestigious Guttman Institute of Applied Social Research, first published in 1993.

An interesting fact is that the so-called secular 20 percent of the Jewish population provides almost all of Israel's leaders in politics, business, the free professions, and academe. They are overwhelmingly from Eastern or Central Europe (immigrants themselves, or descendants of immigrants) as opposed to countries on the Mediterranean rim. This is the segment that is largely responsible—through influence, connections, and language—for Israel's image as a liberal, free, and unfettered society.

Israel's minorities—Arabs, Muslim and Christian, Druze, Circassians, and non-Arab Christians from Armenian to Mormon—each have their own belief systems and religious practices.

The Diaspora-based Jewish Reform and Conservative movements also contribute to Israel's religious pluralism, but for the reasons described above have not made much headway in this country.

Kashrut

The effect of all this religion on the visitor is slight and is in general to be found in two areas, that of *Kashrut*, the Jewish dietary laws, and that of observance of the Sabbath (*Shabbat*). In addition to the prohibition of all pork products, shellfish, and any other fish without scales, the dietary laws require the strict separation of meat and milk in the kitchen and on the table. No dairy product may be served after meat. Kosher restaurants serve either meat or dairy menus, which means that after a meat meal you cannot have real ice cream or cream with your dessert or milk in your coffee.

Hotels in religious areas follow the dietary laws to the letter. Hotel breakfasts are traditionally milk-based, so if you expect to find any meat products on the breakfast table you will be disappointed. Most tourists find that the lavish Israeli breakfast buffet, with its abundance of salads, cheeses, eggs, smoked fish, breads, pastries, and dairy delicacies offers more than enough, but those craving bacon can find nonkosher restaurants without difficulty near hotels and in areas frequented by tourists.

Strict Sabbath Observance

Shabbat commences at sunset on Friday evening and ends at sunset on Saturday. For the religious, the Sabbath is a day of rest, and no driving, cooking, or work of any kind is permitted—no answering of telephones, no switching on or off of lights or other electrical equipment. One may not even press a button to summon an elevator. In hotels an electronically programmed Shabbat elevator moves up and down automatically, stopping at every floor, throughout the day. There is no public transportation (except in Haifa), and shops remain shut until dusk, apart from a few in shopping outlets outside the cities. But the beaches are open, as are most places of entertainment, cafés, clubs, and nonkosher restaurants. In Jerusalem acess to certain areas may be blocked by the ultra-Orthodox.

So don't expect to travel by bus or train on Saturday, don't plan a shopping expedition for

Saturday, and don't be surprised if your religious friends or business associates don't call you or answer their own phones on a Saturday.

FAMILY LIFE

In Israeli society traditional gender roles, where women are wives and mothers and men are the primary breadwinners, are still perceived as the ideal. Despite the fact that dual-income families are common, with a high percentage of women in the labor force working to contribute to their family's standard of living, fewer women than men actually strive to pursue independent careers. And even in the case of those women who earn high salaries, hold top positions in their professions or corporations, or own their own businesses, it is still the woman in the family who is responsible for household management and bringing up the children. The emancipated man will "help" with these chores.

In spite of this ideal, people are marrying later, divorce is on the rise, family size is shrinking (except among the religious), premarital sexual relations are by and large accepted by the loosely traditional and the secular, and unmarried couples living together have become common. With the emphasis on the importance of having children and on increased financial independence for women, the number of single-parent families is growing, and there is little stigma attached to these, or to same-sex couples.

The family remains a major factor in Israeli life. Friday night is the big night for family gatherings, when children and grandchildren converge on parents and grandparents for the Sabbath meal. Geography helps—because of its size, nowhere in Israel is too far to make the journey for the Shabbat get-together, and in some cases (especially in the case of the religious who don't drive on Shabbat) the family will sleep over. The gathering may be held at different family members' houses, and friends, visitors, and extended family are often invited.

In secular homes the get-together may be for lunch on Friday or brunch on Saturday. Non-religious families often meet for lunch at a restaurant on Saturdays, and a familiar sight over the weekend is that of long tables with guests shouting at each other from one end to the other, and children running around. The weekend get-togethers are repeated on the Jewish holidays.

Grandparents often play a role in helping with children, taking them to and from school, friends, and after-school activities, and, of course, babysitting, as well as giving financial support. Exchanging presents is ongoing, with Israelis giving generous gifts to celebrate every occasion.

TOGETHERNESS AND GROUPS

It is a great compliment to be called a *hevreman* (an outgoing, sociable person). A gregarious people, Israelis form deep and lasting friendships, at school, in the neighborhood, but most importantly in the army, where the quality of loyalty is ingrained. After army service many youngsters travel together to the far corners of the earth. As young couples, married or about to be, they are surrounded by friends, some from her side, some from his. They go on trips (*tiyulim*) to the countryside together, picnic together, go to the beach together, go pubbing together, and eat out at restaurants together. When they have their own homes they entertain the *hevre* (their circle of friends) at coffee and cake evenings enlivened by jokes, political arguments, and the swapping of recent experiences, good and bad. They go skiing, charter yachts, and go camping with the children together. Newcomers to the group are warmly welcomed, but unless they have something special to contribute, are soon ignored. Israelis are bad at introductions.

The old boys' network, built and maintained by group friendships, results in widespread "jobs for pals" favoritism, in government, municipalities, public utilities, fully or partially state-owned monopolies, and business generally.

ATTITUDES TOWARD EACH OTHER

On the macro level Israelis have a high regard for each other, and few things give an Israeli more pleasure than a fellow countryman's success. As a nation they regard themselves as being flexible, resourceful, generous, direct, patriotic, courageous, warm, and easy to please. On the other hand, they acknowledge that they may be overconfident, bad listeners, a bit abrasive, risk takers, and even somewhat lawless, traits that they don't regard as particularly important anyway.

On the micro level it is quite different, and other than toward those in their inner circle, Israelis tend to be competitive, judgmental, and critical of each other. They rarely pay compliments or give credit to each other, and there is a Hebrew expression "*simha l'ed*" that describes the pleasure derived from another's misfortune. Epithets such as stupid (*tipesh, metumtam, idiot*), sucker (*freier*), crook (*ganav*), and madman (*meshugah*) are freely used to describe their fellows without compunction. Because of the pressures of life in this beleaguered country and the tensions they produce, negative first impressions are often hastily formed.

Other factors influence the attitudes of Israelis toward each other. The older generations still retain their pre-immigration prejudices, with Lithuanians looking down on Poles and vice versa; German Jews feeling superior to everyone else and being regarded as rigid and snobbish in return; Western newcomers condescending to those from the East, and so on through the different backgrounds of those who make up the ethnic mosaic of the country.

Selfishness and Selflessness

Egocentricity is part of the Israeli character, and most Israelis show varying degrees of competitiveness. They don't suffer fools gladly, and the gullible are scorned. In the early years of the State, this trait was to some extent contained by the prevailing socialist and egalitarian ethos, but with the dissipation of those ideals it became every man for himself, "*Im ayn ani li, mi li?*" ("If I am not for myself, who will be for me?") In times of national crisis, however, this attitude immediately gives way to selfless cooperation, and Israeli solidarity becomes impenetrable.

In Israel, Ashkenazim, those Jews originating in Central and Eastern Europe—whose liturgy follows the German (*Ashkenaz*) rite—are ambivalent toward the Sephardim—who follow the liturgical rite of Spain (*Sepharad*)—who came mainly from Arab and Muslim lands; and these

Sephardim don't have much love for the Ashkenazim, and in fact have a history of grievances against them.

Sabras, native-born Israelis, have on the rational level largely abandoned their parents' prejudices, but in cases of confrontation the old attitudes can bubble to the surface. Also the many areas of contention, particularly in politics and religion, and in many areas the high density of population made up of people of different backgrounds with different norms of behavior, can lead to friction that would be absent in more spacious and homogeneous environments.

On the other hand, Israelis tend not to harbor grievances, are quickly willing to change their unfavorable first impressions, to try again, to forgive and forget, and make friends.

ATTITUDES TOWARD MINORITIES

Attitudes toward Israel's minorities vary. They are generally amicable toward non-Arab Christians, Druze, and Circassians. Toward Israeli Arabs, they run the gamut from suspicion and distrust on the part of the Ashkenazim to dislike and sometimes outright hatred on the part of many of the Sephardim originating in Arab countries where Jews were persecuted. Christian Israeli Arabs on the whole come off better.

Despite the ongoing conflict in the region, which complicates relationships between Jews and Arabs, there is a surprising amount of warm interaction between Arab and Jewish businessmen, Arab restaurateurs and shopkeepers and their clients, and Arab and Jewish coworkers in tourism, agriculture, industry, and commerce. In the arts, media, and elsewhere—particularly in the numerous associations and interfaith projects where Jewish and Arab Israelis, and even Palestinians, work together for common causes, including peace, plurality, human rights, and democracy—Arabs and Jews form deep friendships. The Intifadas have, unfortunately, polarized attitudes among the young.

A Generous Gesture

Invited to a Muslim wedding ceremony by an Arab Israeli notable, the Jewish guests at the reception were surprised and impressed when, seated at tables with other Jewish guests, they were given baskets containing bottles of wine and whiskey by the male members of the host's family, even though according to Islam alcohol is strictly forbidden. "Celebrate with us in your own way," said the father of the groom, their gracious host.

HUMOR

Humor is the great defense mechanism. Throughout their history, laughter has helped the Jews survive disaster, and enabled them to cope with everyday hardships. The basis of Jewish humor is "*Hochmat Haim*" (the wisdom of life), and is universal. Jews laugh at themselves, at life's absurdities, and at man's frailties. Israeli humor is more esoteric. Masters at last in their own land, Israelis laugh more at everyday situations and less at the universal human condition. Their jokes tend to be based on the political, social, and economic situation, current events, and people. Every new wave of immigrants is grist to the humor mill; today's news is tomorrow's joke. Israelis are excellent satirists and in the secular Israeli world nothing is sacred. They prefer to laugh at others rather than at themselves. They enjoy making fun of each other, their pretensions, their ethnic backgrounds, their idols, and their credos. Television programs and print media parody corruption in government, sports, big business, the military. Nothing is sacrosanct. Slapstick comedy is popular, as is sexual innuendo.

chapter three

CUSTOMS & TRADITIONS

JEWISH FESTIVALS AND PUBLIC HOLIDAYS
Jewish festivals are celebrated according to the
Hebrew calendar—consisting of twelve lunar
months set in the framework of a solar year—and
not according to the Gregorian calendar. All
Jewish festivals begin at sunset on the preceding
day and end at dusk on the holiday.

The Days of Awe
Rosh ha-Shanah: the Jewish New Year
Usually falling in September, the two-day New Year's
festival initiates ten days of penitence and soul-
searching. The liturgy describes God as a heavenly
king sitting on His throne and determining the
destiny of each individual in the year ahead. Prayers
of repentance are for mercy and a "good" new year,
and in order to show trust in His compassion, Jews
celebrate the festival with joy. As on the Sabbath,
business in Israel closes down over the Rosh ha-
Shanah holiday. After attending synagogue with the
traditional sounding of the Shofar, the Ram's Horn,

families get together for a sumptuous evening meal.
The candles have been lit at sunset when the festival
begins, and the table is bedecked with apples,
pomegranates, and honey, which symbolize a happy,
fruitful, and sweet year. Families exchange gifts and
New Year cards and e-mail messages are sent out
prior to the holiday to friends and business
acquaintances. "*Shana tova*" ("a good year") is the
traditional greeting.

Yom Kippur: the Day of Atonement
Eight days after Rosh ha-Shanah is Yom Kippur,
the holiest day in the Jewish year, a
day of fasting, prayer, confession,
and repentance of past sins both
against God and against one's fellow men.
From its commencement at dusk until the
appearance of the first stars the next night,
everything shuts down for twenty-five hours,
including radio and television, and the roads are
clear of cars. Synagogues are crowded. No one
drives on Yom Kippur, and children from secular
families come out in droves to cycle with impunity
down the normally traffic-filled streets. Hotels
serve a limited room service menu to guests who
are not fasting. The traditional greeting is "*Gmar
Hatima Tova*," which means, roughly, "May you be
well inscribed in the Book of Life." The evening
service ends with the blowing of the Shofar.

Sukkot

Five days after Yom Kippur the happiest of the biblical festivals, Sukkot, the feast of Tabernacles, celebrates God's bounty and protection. It celebrates the Exodus from Egypt and the ingathering of the fall harvest, the start of the agricultural year, and the first rains. To commemorate the temporary shelters the Israelites dwelt in when they wandered in the desert, throughout Israel thousands of *sukkot* (tabernacles) spring up. These are simple, boothlike structures roofed with palm fronds, citron, myrtle sprigs, and willow branches, in which families gather and in which all meals are eaten until the next festival, Simhat Torah, eight days later (see below). During this period schools are closed and many shops and businesses operate half days. The traditional greeting is *Hag Sameah*, "Happy holiday."

Simhat Torah

This holiday, the "rejoicing of the Law," celebrates the conclusion of the annual reading of the Torah (the five books of Moses) and the renewal of the Torah reading cycle. A feature of this festival is the joyful dancing of orthodox and religious Jews with Torah scrolls in their arms, while chanting the concluding chapters

of Deuteronomy and the opening chapters of
Genesis. Children are given sweets at the
conclusion of the synagogue services.

At this time of the year Israelis talk about
"before" or "after the *hagim* (holidays)." Little is
done before; everything is postponed until after. So
if you plan a business trip between Rosh ha-Shana
and Simhat Torah, take this into consideration.

Hanukkah

Hanukkah, the postbiblical festival of lights,
usually falls in December. It celebrates
the victory of the Jews under the leadership of
the Maccabees in the second century BCE over the
Greek Seleucids, who had desecrated the
Jerusalem Temple. The festival lasts for eight days
and is marked by the nightly lighting of candles
to commemorate the miracle of the Temple, when
a small supply of sacramental olive oil, only
sufficient to rekindle the Temple *menorah*

(candelabrum) for one day, lasted for eight days.
Schools are closed but otherwise business is as
usual. Every evening families and friends gather
for the candle-lighting ceremony, one candle for
the first night, two for the second, until the last
night when the *hanukiah*, the eight-branched
candle holder, is a splendid sight with
all eight candles alight. There are
holiday songs and traditional goodies
fried in oil, such as doughnuts and
potato *latkes* (fritters), are served.
Children are given presents,
typically a spinning top (*dreidl*)
and coins ("*hanukkah gelt*").

Purim

Purim falls in early spring, usually in March.
Everyone's, especially the children's, favorite festival,
it celebrates the deliverance of the Jews in Persia in
the fifth century BCE by Esther, the beautiful Jewish
queen of King Ahasuerus (Xerxes I), and her cousin
Mordecai, from the genocidal plans of the evil
prime minister Haman. Merriment is mandatory
on Purim. To show that things are not what they
seem, and that God works in mysterious ways, fancy
dress and parody of authority are permitted, with
children and often adults dressed up in colorful
Purim costumes turning the streets into a Mardi
Gras. Three-cornered buns known as *hamantaschen*

are eaten. There are fancy dress parties at schools and in homes, and the countryside, bright with spring flowers, is filled with picnicking families and friends.

Pesah (Passover)

This important festival usually falls in April. Celebrated by religious and secular alike, Passover commemorates the redemption of the Children of Israel from their bondage in Egypt. The weeklong festival, during which schools are closed and businesses work half days, commences with the ritual Seder meal. On this "night different from any other night," families and extended families gather together for a feast at which the *Hagaddah* text, recounting the Exodus story of slavery and freedom, is read aloud together, and songs of praise are sung to the Lord. No bread, flour, or any other products containing leaven (yeast) may be consumed during Passover, and bread is replaced by *matza*, the unleavened "bread of affliction" eaten by the Israelites in Egypt. Many hotels organize communal Seders for their guests and outside visitors. The last line of the *Hagaddah* promises "Next year in Jerusalem," and Jews worldwide look forward to spending this spring festival in Israel. Passover is understandably Israel's highest tourist season. The first and last days of the festival are public holidays.

Lag ba-Omer

The thirty-third day of the counting of the Omer (sheaf of the new barley harvest), in the seven weeks from Pesah to Shavu'ot, is a festive break in a period of mourning. Weddings are allowed, music is enjoyed, and the devout make a pilgrimage to the tomb of the second-century mystic Simon Bar Yochai, in Meron, near Safed. Bonfires are lit and three-year-old Orthodox boys receive their first haircut.

Shavu'ot

Shavuot (Pentecost) usually falls in May. Originally the festival of the wheat harvest, it celebrates the revelation of the Ten Commandments to Moses on Mount Sinai. This is a joyous holiday when synagogues are decorated with flowers, many kibbutzim put on plays and other forms of entertainment, and children are dressed in white and crowned with floral wreaths. Dairy foods such as blintzes and cheesecake are traditional fare.

Yom ha-Sho'ah (Holocaust Martyrs' and Heroes' Remembrance Day)

Falling shortly after Passover, the day is dedicated to the memory of the six and a half million Jews who perished in the Holocaust, and to those who resisted, whether individually in the camps, in uprisings against the Nazis, or fighting with the partisans. A siren is sounded at 10:00 a.m. and the nation stands to attention and observes two minutes' silence.

Yom ha-Zikaron (Remembrance Day)

A week after mourning the victims of the Holocaust, Israel pays tribute to the sons and daughters who fell in defense of the State. At 8:00 p.m. on the eve of Remembrance Day and at 10:00 a.m. the following morning, sirens are sounded and a two-minute silence is observed. Restaurants and places of entertainment are closed.

Yom ha-Azma'ut (Independence Day)

Celebrations of the anniversary of the proclamation of the state of Israel on May 14, 1948, begin at sunset on the Day of Remembrance. Israel's Independence Day is a true public holiday, a day for parties, trips into the countryside, barbecues and get-togethers. In the early years

 of the state the day was marked by military parades, which have since been replaced by flypasts and naval displays.

MUSLIM AND CHRISTIAN FESTIVALS

For Muslims the most sacred festival is possibly Eid el-Adha, which commemorates Abraham's sacrifice of a ram instead of his son (in the Koran Ismail, rather than Isaac).

Ramadan, the ninth month of the lunar Muslim calendar, is when the Koran was said to have been revealed to the prophet Mohammed by the angel Gabriel. During this month Muslims fast from sunrise to sunset. The end of Ramadan is marked by the three-day feast of Eid el-Fitr. Fridays and the festivals of Islam are recognized as official Muslim holidays.

Christian holidays are celebrated by their communities, with different denominations celebrating the holy days on different dates. Easter and Christmas, are of course, the main festivals. There is a Christian Information Center in Jerusalem.

RITES OF PASSAGE
Brith Milah

A boy is formally named eight days after the birth as part of the ritual of circumcision (*brith milah*). A girl is formally named on the first Sabbath after the birth (*britha*).

On the eighth day after birth the foreskin is removed from the baby boy's penis at a ceremony conducted either at home or in a function hall in the presence of family and friends. The surgery is performed by a *mohel*, a trained ritual circumciser, after which all the guests are invited to partake in a celebratory meal. The word *brith* means pact, or covenant, and the ritual goes back to God's covenant with Abraham and confirms the status of the child as a member of the Jewish people. If the child is premature, or is not well, the *brith* may be postponed. Parties held to celebrate the event range from intimate at-home affairs with family and close friends to catered events. In secular circles it is becoming fashionable to have the *brith* ceremony at home and a party at a later date.

Pidyon ha-Ben ("Redemption of the Son")
This ancient Levitical ritual, confirming that the firstborn son belongs to God, takes place after the child is thirty days old. After the priestly blessing, a party is held to celebrate the occasion.

Bar and *Bat Mitzvah*
On turning thirteen a boy is considered a responsible adult for most religious purposes, and the same applies to a girl when she turns twelve. They are now duty bound to observe the Commandments. In the *bar mitzvah* ceremony that marks this transition the boy is called up to the reading of the Torah. This is an important

milestone in the life of the family. Following the religious ceremony, in the synagogue or at the Western Wall, a *Kiddush* reception is held. The event may also be celebrated at a festive lunch or dinner, to which not only family and friends but also clients, employers, colleagues, professional associates, and acquaintances may be invited. All arrive bearing generous gifts or checks.

Bat mitzvahs are also celebrated, but usually more modestly, often for a number of girls together, and with smaller events.

COURTSHIP AND MARRIAGE

Other than in the case of the ultra-Orthodox, courtship follows much the same pattern as it does elsewhere in the Western world. Boy meets girl, they like each other, date a while, develop an intimate relationship, move in and live together, and finally decide to get married. Or they part and start all over again with someone else.

In the case of the ultra-Orthodox it is quite different. Matchmakers are generally used to introduce young people, and a first meeting takes place in a public area, such as a hotel lobby, or strictly chaperoned, to find out if they are compatible. Over a modest glass of mineral water or Coke they ask each other questions and reveal their aspirations and goals in life. If they feel that they are suited there are further meetings, followed by family negotiations over marriage settlements, and the marriage takes place.

The Marriage Ceremony

The minimum requirement for a religious Jewish marriage (there are no civil marriages in Israel) is a rabbi, a *huppah* (wedding canopy), an exchange of rings, and marriage vows in the presence of two witnesses. The young couple, their parents, and the

rabbi stand under the *huppah*, which is open at the sides and supported by poles at the four corners held by close family members or friends. At the conclusion of the ceremony, after the rings

have been exchanged and the groom has kissed his bride, he stamps on a glass (normally wrapped in a napkin), shattering it—a reminder of the sadness felt at the destruction of the Temple in Jerusalem, or that happiness can never be complete.

The wedding reception is a huge and jolly affair. In the case of the ultra-Orthodox, men and women are separated for both dining and dancing, in the same way as they are separated in the synagogue. These receptions are lavish occasions, and gifts are often extremely generous to help defray the costs when the parents are not well-off.

The costs of the wedding are usually shared by both sets of parents. Venues proliferate, with wedding halls in the cities, outdoors in orchards or orange groves, in kibbutzim, on the seashore, or the fertile coastal plain, often requiring guests to drive long distances to participate. After all the toasts and revelry, driving home is no pleasure. Some young secular couples go abroad to marry in a civil ceremony (Cyprus is a popular destination) and hold a wedding reception on their return home.

DEATH AND MOURNING

Jewish traditions relating to death and mourning have two purposes: to show respect for the dead, and to comfort the living.

The practicalities are attended to by the *hevra kaddisha*, the burial society, whose cemeteries are found throughout the country, some like English graveyards but most with tombstones laid out like soldiers in rows one next to the other; some have shady trees, others not. Nondenominational cemeteries, quite costly, are also spread throughout the country, mostly in the grounds of kibbutzim, where there is greater peace and beauty.

Following the funeral, the bereaved keep seven days of intense mourning, called *shivah*. Parents, children, spouse, and siblings of the deceased gather together, usually in the deceased's home, to give full expression to their grief, and slowly begin the journey back to everyday life. During the seven days, friends, neighbors, relatives, and colleagues call to offer their condolences, many bringing cakes and meals so that the mourners need not bother with cooking.

chapter four

MAKING FRIENDS

We have seen that Israelis like to surround themselves with friends and to move around in groups, and how difficult it is for outsiders to penetrate established circles. This does not, however, mean that Israelis are not open to new friendships; these will exist outside the groups and cater to different needs. Common interests such as sports, hobbies, cultural pursuits, professional and business concerns are all foundations for outside friendships that can prove as enduring and rewarding as those born of common experience. But true friendship to an Israeli is more than simply good company or chemistry. It involves loyalty, investment in time, sometimes inconvenience, and even, in extreme circumstances, personal risk. Both commitment and expectations are high.

HOSPITALITY

Israelis are a warm and hospitable people, proud of their homes and families, who enjoy the role of hosts. Depending on their background, you may be invited to join a family on a Friday night for Shabbat supper; or for another festive occasion; or to meet their friends at a Saturday brunch or barbecue; or for coffee and cake in the late afternoon; or after dinner at night; or you may be invited to a restaurant, pub, or club. Most business entertaining is done outside the home. Israelis love their country and enjoy taking guests around to see the sights and beauty spots.

Invitations Home

Invitations home for dinner could be for any time from 7:00 to 9:00 p.m. Arrive on time, but don't be surprised if you are the first guest, as Israelis are not famed for their punctuality. It is customary to bring a small gift for your hosts (see below), and you'll fit in if you dress in smart casual attire—no ties and suits. It is hard to generalize about what to expect, as there is such diversity in Israel and the hospitality you receive will reflect the customs and traditions of the family. You can expect dinners at the home of Westernized Israelis (both religious and secular) to be similar to what you are accustomed to, with good food and wine and lively conversation.

Israelis are not heavy drinkers, but in most homes you will be offered a drink (usually wine and soft drinks) before dinner, and wine will be served with the meal. Habits are changing and some households do keep spirits and serve predinner cocktails.

Shabbat dinners are usually family affairs, so expect to find children seated at the table and lively conversation. In traditional homes, and many secular homes too, the Shabbat candles will have been lit by the lady of the house at sunset, and the host will recite the traditional Shabbat prayers and blessings before the meal, during which all remain standing.

Table manners are Western style; dishes are passed around, and concern is shown for the guest. In some homes no one will start eating until the guest takes the first bite. So if everyone is served and no one is eating, go ahead and put them out of their misery. Second helpings are offered, the hostess is delighted when these are accepted, and compliments are happily received. When finished, knives and forks are placed neatly side by side on the plate—or otherwise, depending on the upbringing and origin of the guests and family. If there is no household help then it is customary for the guests to help the hosts clear the table.

Once dinner is over, some hosts want their guests to linger until the small hours, and some can't wait for them to go home. This may sound familiar.

Saturday brunches are jolly affairs, usually lasting from around noon until the last guest leaves. They are very informal, so wear jeans and T-shirts and you'll feel at home.

If you are invited for coffee and cake in the late afternoon, that is what you will be served; but if invited for coffee and cake after dinner, skip dinner and arrive hungry! You will be offered an array of delicious food long before the coffee and cakes appear, and your hostess will be quite offended if you refuse her hospitality.

GIFT GIVING

Israelis regard generosity as a prime virtue. No Israeli wants to be labeled a *kamtzan* (mean or miserly person), and this is strongly reflected in the giving of gifts. In the case of wedding, *bar mitzvah*, and anniversary presents, there is a tendency to go overboard in equating the size of the gift with the value of the friendship. Every Israeli understands that his gift may be helpful in defraying the expenses of the event, and in the case of young couples to help them set up their new household, particularly if he gives a check. If a visitor is invited to such an event he should consult an Israeli friend before deciding what to give. In the case of weddings, the couple may have a wedding list, which facilitates the choice.

If you are invited to an Israeli home a modest gift is customary: chocolates, a bottle of wine, fancy soaps, candles, or a specialty item from home will all be appreciated. Flowers are always welcome, and will be doubly appreciated if sent the day before the dinner, saving the hostess the bother of searching for a vase when you arrive.

Unless you know for sure that your hosts do not keep a kosher home, do not risk offending their religious sensibilities by bringing them nonkosher wine or chocolates from abroad. If you know that small children will be present, a little gift (sweets, coloring pens, etc.) will be warmly received.

You should not give gifts to business associates on your first meeting.

MANNERS

Israelis were, and to an extent still are, notorious for their lack of polish. In the egalitarian rough-and-ready pioneer days, and in reaction to the perceived diffidence and timidity of the Diaspora Jew, they dispensed with social niceties and opted for a manly brusqueness. They never allowed themselves to feel like strangers. The legacy of this is that often Israelis treat total strangers with a familiarity usually reserved for members of the family.

No matter where in Israel or with whom, some Israelis never feel like strangers. They feel no compunction about asking someone how much he earns or what he paid for his suit or house. On receiving a reply they may give their opinion: "You earn too little," or "You paid too much." This form of behavior is not considered rude, but rather as a positive example of straightforwardness. "*Doogri*" is the word, and a virtue. They may also not feel the need to apologize when they arrive late. They'll speak loudly on their cell phones at restaurants or while seated in a crowded café, and let their children run wild. They'll drive without consideration, weave in and out of lanes, honk indiscriminately, and when parking occupy two spaces instead of one.

Once upon a time these were behavioral norms in Israel. But no longer. Although still straightforward, today most Israelis, particularly the younger generation, are better educated, more courteous and considerate, do not intrude on your eardrums or space, and place a limit on their straightforwardness.

So there is no reason to be apprehensive. Watch your own manners, for example in the home of an

Orthodox family: if you are a woman dress modestly, and if you are a man don't shake hands with your hostess or hug and kiss her good-bye when you take your leave. In a Muslim home don't show the soles of your feet and don't use your left hand for eating—even if you are left-handed.

IMMIGRANT ASSOCIATIONS

For visitors planning a long stay, it may be helpful to approach an appropriate immigrant association for advice. Associations representing immigrants from more than thirty countries provide their members with support, assistance, and care in matters related to employment, housing, health, and special needs. A few of these associations, such as the AACI (the Associations of Americans and Canadians in Israel) and Telfed (the South African Immigrant Association), have well-staffed offices, publish bimonthly and quarterly magazines, and are supported by donations from the better-off members of their communities. Others work as volunteers to provide services to members who are in need.

The AACI offers counseling, advice on money management, investment, will and trust consultation, and advice on U.S. tax planning. They have a number of support groups, including those for parents of physically and mentally challenged children and for single parents. They run workshops for writers, conditioning exercise classes for women, Feldenkrais, dance and movement, and organize question and answer meetings with lawyers, municipal councillors, and experts in other fields.

Telfed provides job counseling, organizes annual social events and get-togethers, and acts as a link between former South Africans living in Israel.

Both AACI and Telfed, after payment of expenses, distribute their revenues philanthropically. Their income derives from members' dues, gifts, and subscription fees to their magazines, plus support from the Zionist organizations in their country of origin. Work is mostly carried out by volunteers.

The former British Olim Society (BOS), which provided services to immigrants from the United Kingdom, Ireland, Scandinavia, Australia, and New Zealand, has been incorporated into the UJIA Israel, the United Jewish Israel Appeal, through which help in all aspects of the immigration process is offered.

ESRA is an across-the-board philanthropic immigrant association, whose motto is "volunteering together for the community." This diverse and dynamic organization has volunteers who provide English-speaking residents with social, educational, and support activities to help their integration process. It also supplies education, development, social, and welfare programs to those with special needs in the Sharon area and on a national level. Its activities range from divorce mediation to running charity shops, book clubs, sewing centers, cinema clubs, hiking clubs, writers' and poets' circles, singles clubs for all ages, and many others touching on every aspect of life in Israel. Proceeds of donations, membership fees, and ticket sales to cultural, sporting, and other events, shops and special services, are distributed philanthropically. ESRA publishes a glossy quarterly magazine.

The International Women's Club was founded to promote friendship and understanding between the women of the international community (diplomats and expats) and Israeli women through social, cultural, and educational activities. The club is not a fund-raising institution, is not religious, and has no political affiliation. The IWC is a member of the Open Door and the WCI, Welcome Clubs International.

Every new immigrant is entitled to attend an *ulpan* (intensive Hebrew school) for five hours daily, five days a week, for five months, free of charge. Ethiopian immigrants are granted an extra five months. Schooling takes place in absorption centers, on kibbutzim, or in local community centers.

Also, all the major universities allow non-degree candidates to attend special courses for a fee, some of which are in English. The English-Speaking Friends of the Tel Aviv University Association organizes monthly lectures and annual seminars for its members in English and informs them of other lectures and activities in English on the campus in the monthly newsletter.

chapter five

DAILY LIFE

HOMES AND LIFESTYLES

Urban Israelis are in the main apartment
dwellers, although there are many suburban
neighborhoods throughout the country in which
families live in private houses, referred to as
"villas," and two-story town houses, known as
"cottages," surrounded by their own relatively
small gardens. There are also houses built on
large plots of land on moshavim and private
land in the countryside.

Apartments in the suburbs and city vary from
standard to luxurious, depending on their
location and when they were built or renovated.
Most apartments range from two to five rooms

and, including upmarket
housing, their living areas
are relatively large and the
bedrooms small. All
modern buildings have
elevators, but you may find
yourself climbing four
flights of stairs to visit a

friend with an apartment in an old building. Some apartments have balconies, others don't. In the narrow urban streets where apartments tend to overlook each other, the balconies of yesteryear (including those of the Bauhaus buildings) were enclosed with plastic shutters in the sixties to enlarge the living space and increase privacy. In later years builders did away with the balcony altogether to provide more spacious living rooms.

Today the sun terrace is right back in fashion, and can be found in many attractive modern high-rise buildings both in the city and in the suburbs, where they are built on larger tracts of land with uninterrupted views. With the advent of modern air-conditioning the old rule that apartments should have cross-ventilation is often disregarded. The modern residential complexes consist of high-rise luxury apartments with marble ceramic or wooden floors and fitted kitchens. Most have lobbies with porters, health clubs in the basements, and are built far from the bustle of city streets. Many of these luxury complexes are near country clubs with swimming pools, tennis courts, and other sports facilities, and well equipped gyms, offering a wide range of exercise and yoga classes, and children's sports activities and programs.

Lifestyles, of course, vary according to where people live and their economic circumstances—

from spilling out on to the streets to escape
cramped living quarters, eating hummus and pita
and *shwarma* (shaved slices of meat) in little cafés,
and barbecuing in parks, to dining out in chic
restaurants, subscribing to the Philharmonic
Orchestra concerts, to theater and opera
performances, and entertaining and relaxing in
their own comfortable homes. Many Israeli
homes, even in less affluent areas, enjoy some
form of household help (having a good *ozeret*, or
helper, is a concern of most housewives).

Most Israelis aspire to own their own homes,
renting mainly when young and unmarried.

WEEKDAY ROUTINE

Weekdays begin early. School begins at 8:00 a.m.
and the working day starts at 8:30 or 9:00 a.m.
Nursery schools open earlier to oblige working
mothers who drop their children off on their way
to work. On kibbutzim and moshavim the
abundant Israeli breakfast is still served, but most
city dwellers give their children a bowl of cereal
and a hot or cold drink and pack a midday snack
for them to take to school. Adults tend to have tea
or coffee with bread rolls and spreads and a
yogurt for breakfast, or munch a granola health
bar in the car on the way to work. The athletic rise
even earlier for early morning jogging, walking, or

swimming, and can be seen marching briskly around the neighborhood at dawn or exercising on the beach or in the parks.

The working day ends at 5:00 or 5:30 p.m., but lawyers, high-tech, and managerial staff in every area will leave the office much later. After work, for those who have time, there are enrichment courses (anything from learning massage techniques to business, music, and academic courses); entertaining and being entertained, going to the movies, or other cultural events; shopping in malls, markets, main streets, and all-night supermarkets. Many will seize the chance to have a nap after work before setting off for a restaurant, pub, club, or café. Visitors are always amazed to see the streets of Tel Aviv alive till the early hours of the morning right throughout the week.

Working parents come home late, and working mothers especially devote most of their free time to the children, helping with their homework and other routine tasks, and spending quality time with them before their bedtime. For many working mothers Friday is a day off, and in the mornings they may have some time for themselves. At noon they pick up the children and go home for lunch and a siesta before getting ready for the Shabbat family dinner and the weekend.

Daily life in Israel is accompanied by the pressures of reserve duty; of having children serving in the army, and not knowing at any given time what they are doing and if they are in any danger; of the high level of taxation, which presents a particular challenge to the self-employed—and of keeping up with the latest trends.

EDUCATION

Jewish mothers everywhere boast of their children's educational achievements and Israel is no exception. Education is a core value, with every generation bent on maintaining or raising the level. From the moment a baby is born, the proud parents plan his future. There are DVDs and special toys to develop intelligence; children's computer programs, private preschool English-language classes, and so on, and many parents gladly sacrifice their own comforts and standard of living to provide their children with the highest standard of education.

The visitor to Israel may wonder at the sight of children from the age of five or six trudging to school under the weight of heavy backpacks containing their books and other school supplies. Israeli schools have no lockers. Why? Perhaps finance, who knows? This may be one of the reasons so many adults suffer from back problems in Israel.

Because of other demands, mostly defense, paradoxically for a people who place such emphasis on schooling, government budgets for education are generally accepted as being woefully inadequate. Teachers are underpaid and many schools, particularly in poor areas, suffer from a lack of amenities, including computers, and poor maintenance.

For youngsters under the age of five, day care centers are available but optional, and, apart from some that are subsidized, not free. From five or six until the age of sixteen, education is compulsory, and is free until the age of eighteen. Schools in Israel are mostly coeducational, with boys and girls studying together from the stage where they find the opposite sex "so annoying" till the age when they find them anything but.

"Free" does not mean free books, paper, pens, pencils, uniforms where required (mostly T-shirts bearing the school's logo, and jeans), transportation if needed, school trips, non-curricular courses, after-school programs, or of course the ubiquitous schoolbag.

There is a view that the best education and formative training is provided in the *gan hova* (compulsory preschool for five-year-olds). Dedicated and well trained teachers (*gannanot*) do a great job, particularly in the area of self-esteem at this critical stage of their young wards' lives.

Primary school follows from first to eighth grade. There are two official tracks for this group—secular (traditional) and religious. There are also separate state schools for Arabs and Druze, where instruction is in Arabic. The devoutly orthodox Jewish community have their own schools, differing according to the nuances of their observances, some partially and some fully government funded. The divergence between secular and religious Israelis now becomes more pronounced, with the religious often required to sleep in or become boarders at high school. There are a few private schools where the medium of instruction is English or another language: the Walworth Barbour American International School in Kfar Shemariyahu; Tabeetha, the Church of Scotland school in Jaffa; and the French School in Jaffa (Collège de Frères). In high school pupils select the stream in which they wish to continue their studies—academic, technological, agricultural, or military. Corporal punishment is forbidden at schools in Israel.

Over recent years there has been a disturbing increase in deviant behavior in schools—violence and drug abuse—which may be caused by high unemployment, the growing gap between rich and poor, and, among the unemployed, the diminished status of the father as a role model.

For high-school graduates there are seven main institutions of advanced learning: the Hebrew University of Jerusalem, Tel Aviv University, Bar

Ilan University, Haifa University, Ben Gurion University of the Negev, the Technion Institute of Technology in Haifa, and the Weizmann Institute of Science in Rehovot. None of these are free, and all students other than those with scholarships have to pay for their own tuition. In addition to these there are private colleges that have been accredited to award degrees. Admission is easier, but they are more expensive than the universities.

Although higher education has greatly contributed to the growth and development of the country, with more than 200,000 students currently enrolled in its various academic institutions, most Israeli postgraduates have little nostalgia for their university days and alumni associations hold little allure. This is perhaps because Israeli students enroll at university at the age that students elsewhere have already completed their undergraduate studies, and have to work so hard to pay their relatively high university fees that they have no time to enjoy a full campus life. After three tough years in the army, many take a year off, and backpack around the world, especially to South and Central America, India, and Thailand. These begin their university studies even later.

Minimum admission requirements are the Israeli matriculation certificate, the *bagrut*, or its equivalent, attaining the required standard in the psychometric exam, and proficiency in Hebrew to cope with the courses. Certain faculties require Israeli citizenship for admission. There are programs to help students reach the required level of Hebrew proficiency.

LEISURE AND SPORTS

Leisure activities have been touched upon, but there are some interests that are common to the majority of Israelis, no matter what their lifestyle. One of these is soccer. Israeli men are passionate soccer fans, following the fortunes of their chosen teams and not allowing anything to interfere with live broadcasts of national and international matches. Next to soccer comes basketball.

Another passion is reading the daily newspapers. There are more papers published and read per capita in Israel than anywhere else in the world. Most print media is in Hebrew, but there are also English, Russian, French, German, and other foreign-language publications. They are read at home, in cafés, on buses, on airplanes, at beaches, and on benches in all public areas. Keeping up with the ever-changing news is vital, and in addition to the print media there are radio and television channel broadcasts on the hour throughout the day and in the evenings. The evening news programs on Channels One, Two, and Ten dominate the air (see Chapter 9).

Israelis love card games and usually play for money. Bridge, poker, and 21 are popular, as are the board games backgammon (*shesh besh*) and chess. There are chess centers throughout the country. In Israel there are 4,500 chess players participating in organized leagues, while 10,000 other players take part in school and club competitions. The Kasparov Chess Center near Tel Aviv University's campus, donated by former world champion Gary Kasparov, teaches chess teachers.

For those Israelis who can afford it, travel is high on the agenda. The well-off travel to Europe and long-haul destinations, and those with smaller budgets go to Cyprus, the Greek Islands, Turkey, and Eastern Europe. Post-army youths, as we have seen, backpack for months at a time to the four corners of the globe.

Thai Break
It is said that because of the large numbers of Israelis visiting Thailand, many Thais think Israel must be the largest country in the world.

chapter six

TIME OUT

Jewish festivals revolve around food, including the traditional delicacies with symbolic associations. Today even Independence Day has become synonymous with the yearly *mengel*, an outdoor barbecue in gardens, parks, the countryside, or wherever space is available.

Over the years, tastes and habits have changed. Traditional Jewish foods are still enjoyed at festival meals, but are less often prepared at home by the average housewife, who lacks both time and inclination to spend long hours in the kitchen. Dishes such as gefilte fish, chopped liver, cholent, kube, hummus, tahina, and stuffed vegetables are picked up from the deli or enjoyed at a grandparent's home. Climate and health have also played their role, and Mediterranean cuisine, using olive oil and fresh herbs, is everywhere.

WINING AND DINING
Israel is awash with restaurants. The weekly English edition of *Ha'aretz* magazine

recommends and reviews those specializing in different cuisines: Far Eastern, Fish and Seafood, French, Italian, Jewish, Meat, Middle Eastern and Balkan, Spanish, and various others.

Just as the Jewish homeland needed Jewish farmers to become a normal country, it also needed Jewish chefs. In the early years of the State virtually the only restaurants to be found were family owned and operated, offering the traditional fare of the many countries from which Israelis had emigrated. Sons and daughters helped to serve and wash the dishes in these "hole in the wall" eateries, and many have carried on running them, bringing them up-to-date with contemporary décor and modern equipment to cater to a more sophisticated clientele. The "boat people," refugees taken in by Israel after the war in Vietnam, and their progeny, were the first to offer, and continue to provide, a taste of the Far East.

In recent years a culinary revolution has taken place. A new generation of talented young Israeli chefs, many of whom were apprenticed to Italian and French chefs in Michelin-starred restaurants, others of whom traveled abroad and absorbed the culinary traditions of East and West, has emerged in Israel, and together with local entrepreneurs, they have opened restaurants that compete on all levels with their counterparts in Rome, Paris, London, and New York. A contributing influence to this culinary renaissance is an insatiable thirst for travel. The hundreds of thousands of Israelis who travel abroad for business and pleasure each year return with a sharpened awareness of quality, including an appreciation of fine cuisine that was nonexistent in the early years. Today the ever-growing number of food magazines, columns, reviews, and restaurant articles in the daily and weekend press and the popular TV food shows testify to the new interest in cuisine.

Of the restaurants reviewed by *Ha'aretz*, only twenty-two are kosher, many of which are in hotels. The magazine also reviews about twenty cafés, out of literally thousands, that mostly serve dairy-based dishes with a standard selection of sandwiches, salads, and quiches. Of the cafés reviewed six are kosher.

Most restaurants offer breakfast menus including fresh orange juice, smoked fish, salads, cheeses, eggs, coffee, and teas, and fixed-price business-lunch menus offering good meals that are less expensive than dinners. Generally, both local and imported wines are available, local and imported spirits, and a choice of beers and soft drinks. Upmarket establishments also offer a range of cocktails.

There are restaurants on the beaches, in malls, in the main shopping streets, alongside fishing harbors and marinas, and in picturesque spots in the countryside. A current popular location is the old Tel Aviv harbor at the northwestern end of downtown Tel Aviv. Mediterranean fish and vegetable dishes are plentiful, with good cuts of meat a more expensive option. One specialty is the delicious St. Peter's fish from the Sea of Galilee.

Arab restaurants are to be found mostly in Jerusalem, Jaffa, in and around Haifa, and in the Galilee, where some of the restaurants are Druze, serving traditional Arab, or so-called "Oriental," cuisine. In this the *mezze*, consisting of a dizzying selection of spicy salads and dips, including tahina and hummus, plays a prominent role.

Other than in hotels, in Arab and Druze restaurants, and in Far Eastern restaurants, there are few career waiters in Israeli establishments. Service is provided mainly by students, who rely on tips to help them through university or college.

Smoking is usually permitted at bar counters and in outside areas.

TIPPING

In restaurants, 12 to 15 percent of the bill is usual. A service charge may already be included. Exceptional service may deserve a little more.

In hotels, bellboys are usually tipped the equivalent of U.S. $1 per suitcase. Room service waiters always expect a tip. It is usual to leave an envelope enclosing a tip for the housekeeping staff and front office personnel at the desk on departure.

Taxi drivers appreciate tips, but do not expect them. Tourist guides and drivers do expect them.

Gas station attendants appreciate a small tip for good service.

SHOPPING

In Israel shopping is a national hobby. Israelis shop in the malls, in the main streets, in the markets, at outlets in industrial areas, in airport duty-free shops when traveling, or in the airport mall before meeting or greeting friends—even at hospitals, where retail therapy takes on a different meaning for shoppers in the malls that have sprung up in the hospital grounds or adjacent to them. There are rustic arts and crafts studios and boutiques in country villages, and fashionable boutiques in seaside port developments. Israelis are price conscious and will shop around for the best buy. Prices are fixed, and there is little opportunity for bargaining in shops.

Miles of Malls

Until fairly recently malls were unknown in Israel. Today, both in the cities and on their outskirts, malls are attracting customers who prefer to do their shopping in air-conditioned comfort, with parking and all the shops they need. Some malls are more sophisticated than others, but most have entertainment for children, cinema complexes, cafés, and fast-food emporiums, branches of fashion chains for adults and children, electronic goods suppliers, supermarkets, video and DVD shops for sales and rentals, bookshops, toy shops, shoe shops, and cell phone suppliers. A few have bowling alleys and some open on Saturdays. Many feature prepared food fairs on Friday mornings.

Markets

Shukim (singular, *shuk*) are open-air markets. With their abundance of fresh fruits and vegetables they attract not only frugal shoppers but anyone seeking the best produce. It is hard to resist trays of strawberries and ripe tomatoes, crisp green lettuces and herbs, pungent pickles, piles of spices, endless varieties of olives, salads,

breads, meat, and fish, and
colorful bunches of
flowers. Faithful customers
enjoy bargaining with the
vendors and buy groceries,
household products,
clothing, accessories, and
toys here. These are much
cheaper, but are not always
the best quality. The

Carmel in Tel Aviv and Mahaneh Yehudah in
Jerusalem are two of the largest markets. In Tel
Aviv on Tuesdays and Fridays there is an arts and
crafts market in Nachalat Benyamin Street, which
is near the Carmel Market, so you can visit both
places in one outing.

FASHION

Israeli women keep up-to-date with the latest
fashion trends in Israel, Milan, Paris, London, and
New York. Those who can buy the labels in
expensive boutiques or outlets, and those who
can't buy good-quality copies in the popular
chains, or shoddy versions in the cheaper shops,
markets, and bazaars.

Israelis tend to exaggerate, and fashion is no
exception. When the look calls for belly-baring, or
body-hugging T-shirts, the youthful, slim, and

shapely wear them with flair, and the older, fatter, and less shapely wear them proudly, too.

Today young Israeli designers are at the cutting edge of fashion and many have made it to the top, with boutiques in Paris, London, and New York. Doreen Frankfort, Bracha Baron, Sigal Dekel, and Ronnit Chen are as well known in international fashion circles today as those of the fashion and swimwear houses Gottex and Gideon Oberson.

Well-dressed Israeli men follow the latest trends in the cut of their trousers, jeans, jackets, shirts, and style of shoe, and aspire to buy the right labels, real or imitation.

Israeli jewelry is distinctive. Handcrafted pieces are made with gold, silver, and precious and semiprecious stones, and sometimes incorporate ancient Roman glass, Jewish coins, and exotic woods. Designs are modern or based on ethnic design, and some use beads and polymer clay.

Israeli beauty services are on a high level, well priced by international standards, and used by most of the population. Like fashion boutiques, hairdressing and beauty salons can be found at every price level, providing manicures, pedicures, and facial and body treatments for men and women. Whereas in colder climes a tan is often a status symbol, in today's Israel the opposite is true; basking in the hot sun is out and hats, sunshades, and protective sun lotions are in.

THE PERFORMING ARTS
Theater

In any given week there are as many as eighty
theatrical productions showing in about forty
theaters or other venues in Israel. Of these, nearly
sixty are playing at twenty theaters in Tel Aviv. The
Habimah National Theater (founded in Moscow by
Nachum Zemach in 1917 and moved to Israel in
1931) and the New Cameri Theater are both
repertory companies that change plays several times
a week. Productions range from translations of
overseas hits, including major musicals, and classics,

 to plays and musicals by
Israeli playwrights dealing
with local and universal
themes. The Cameri stages a
weekly production with
simultaneous English translation. Generally the
curtain rises at 8:30 p.m.

Music

More than twenty classical music concerts can be
heard in any week. Venues include churches and
the two main concert halls, the Mann
Auditorium in Tel Aviv, home of the Israel
Philharmonic Orchestra, and Jerusalem's
International Convention Center, Heichal
Hatarbut. Renowned guest musicians and famous

Israeli soloists—Pinchas Zuckerman, Shlomo Mintz, Daniel Barenboim, and Itzhak Perlman—are part of the country's music scene. Operas are performed at the Tel Aviv Center of Performing Arts at different times throughout the year, and in summer at the restored Roman amphitheater in Caesarea.

Israel has a rich heritage of folk and popular music. Past and present songwriters, singers, and composers include Naomi Shemer, Shoshana Damari, Ehud Banai, Yafa Yarkoni, Arik Einstein, Shalom Chanoch, David Broza, and Achinoam Nini, among many others. Israeli popular song embraces nostalgia for the early days of the country, its wars, triumphs, and losses; songs of heroism, dreams of peace, songs of simple pleasures, and of the frustrations of everyday life, and love songs that pull at the heart.

Dance

Local and foreign dance companies perform classical ballet and modern dance at venues throughout Israel, including the Suzanne Dellal Center in Neveh Tzedek, Tel Aviv, home of the Bat Sheva Ballet Company. Ballet is also performed at the Roman amphitheater in Caesarea.

Israelis are enthusiastic folk dancers, and there are folk dance groups throughout the country.

Other Entertainment

All kinds of performances take place throughout the country. Shows include dance, poetry, drama, jazz, progressive rock, operetta, satire, stand-up comedy, cabaret, Israeli popular music, and Russian and Gospel singers. There are also circuses, puppet shows, and children's programs of all kinds. Most adult performances start at 9:00 p.m. and take place in small theaters, café-bars, clubs, centers, and auditoriums. There are many performances in English and other languages.

MUSEUMS AND GALLERIES

In addition to the three main museums with their permanent and special exhibitions—the Israel Museum in Jerusalem, the Tel Aviv Museum of Art, and the Haaretz Museum in Tel Aviv—there are more than eighty museums and art galleries scattered throughout Israel. These have individual and group exhibits of sculpture, painting, and works of all kinds by known and unknown artists. Worth a detour is the charming artists' village of Ein Hod in the Carmel foothills near Haifa, the Artists' Quarter in Old Jaffa, and Safed in the Galilee. Gordon Street in Tel Aviv has a concentration of galleries offering a wide variety of Israeli art. Three of the most well-attended museums are listed below; details of others may easily be found on the Internet and elsewhere.

The Holon Children's Museum
An exciting museum with interactive exhibits.

Beit Hatefutsot (The Museum of the Diaspora)
Situated on the campus of Tel Aviv University, this unique institution shows the history of the different Jewish communities around the world through scale models, architecture, drawings and sketches, multimedia, and artifacts.

Yad Vashem
The Yad Vashem Museum of the Holocaust is situated on Har ha-Zikaron (The Mount of Remembrance) in Jerusalem. It documents the history of the Jewish people during the Holocaust period, preserving the memory and story of the six million victims, and imparting the legacy of the Holocaust for generations to come through its archives, library, school, museums, and recognition of the Righteous Among the Nations.

CULTURAL FESTIVALS
More than seventy cultural festivals are held annually throughout the country. The following is a small selection.

The Jerusalem Festival features international and Israeli theater, dance, and music, with the participation of internationally renowned artists.

Classical and Jazz music festivals take place on kibbutzim (including Kfar Blum, and the Keshet Eilon Violin Mastercourse), at the Red Sea (Jazz festival), the Dead Sea, and the Sea of Galilee.

Several festivals are devoted to choral music, including Jerusalem's Liturgica, vocal music in the churches of Abu Ghosh, and the Zimriya festival.

The annual summer **Akko Festival of Alternative Israeli Theater** is held within the walls of the old Crusader city of Acre.

The **Safed Klezmer** (Jewish Soul Music) Festival attracts both religious and secular young people.

Other events include annual film festivals, screening local and foreign films, in Tel Aviv, Haifa, and Jerusalem; the Karmi'el Dance Festival; Jaffa Nights, outdoor theater and music; the International Poets' Festival; the International Jerusalem Book Fair; the Arthur Rubinstein International Piano Master Competition; and the International Festival of Puppet Theater in Jerusalem.

NIGHTLIFE

Bars and clubs proliferate, mainly in Tel Aviv. The choice ranges from rock music for a young hip crowd, through a small, intimate bar or wine bar with a regular clientele, to a place where "pickup" is the object. You can enjoy an evening of Irish ambience; indulge yourself with a sunset drink after a soothing massage; or choose the places with the best DJs. Some pubs and clubs offer live music and entertainment, others, more sedate, quiet corners and low lighting. There is something for every taste.

BEACHES

From Ashkelon in the south to beyond Nahariya in the north, Israel's coastline consists of a succession of beaches. Most are broad, white, and sandy, some narrow and rocky, and a few are simply sheltered coves. Those falling under local authority or kibbutz supervision are well maintained and clean, have lifeguards, and post safety signs. White flags signify a calm sea, red flags caution against strong waves and currents, and black flags warn that swimming is dangerous and prohibited. Swimming areas are often roped off, creating a corridor in the sea, so that the lifeguards can better keep an eye on their charges.

Officially, bathing is forbidden at any beach without lifeguards in attendance. There can be undertows, strong currents, and uneven ground, and swimming can be dangerous, particularly after dark.

There are shaded areas, and deck chairs and umbrellas for rent. Beachside restaurants, cafés, and kiosks serve meals, drinks, and snacks, and on weekends and holidays vendors ply along the sands selling ice cream, cool drinks, and snacks. Toilets are generally clean and sanitary. There are open-air showers. Tended beaches are crowded in the late summer afternoons and evenings, over weekends, public holidays, and from morning to night in July and August.

Some beaches are bordered by promenades or landscaped gardens, others simply by parking lots, sand dunes, and scrub. Some are free, others charge everyone entrance fees, and others charge only those who are nonresidents of the authority in question. Some charge parking fees only.

Those beaches that are unattended, often the most wild and beautiful, may be littered by debris, washed ashore or left behind by messy picnickers. Volunteers clear them from time to time.

In addition to the long, wide, sandy beach and promenade that borders Tel Aviv's main hotel and tourist district, North Tel Aviv has beaches with separate appeal, including a segregated beach for the ultra-Orthodox and one for dog owners. (Pets are not allowed onto most attended beaches.) There are unsupervised nudist beaches both north and south of Tel Aviv.

Most tended beaches are dedicated to the peaceful enjoyment of bathers and sunseekers, and do not allow the noisy jet and water-skiing activities offered at other Mediterranean resorts, but many have areas set aside for volleyball and other beach games. Topless bathing on Israel's beaches is generally permitted, but in fact is rarely done except in Eilat.

There are no privately owned beaches; however on the Sea of Galilee many developers of lakeside beach clubs, hotels, and holiday villages have unlawfully fenced in their properties right down to the waters' edge, leaving little beach space available to the public. Many clubs, hotels, and holiday villages offer water sports facilities, and over weekends and holidays the calm blue waters of the Sea of Galilee teem with Jet Skis and other propeller-driven craft, including large, double-decker cruisers ferrying tourists and pilgrims to the holy sites. Sailing boats and wooden fishing boats dot the horizon.

Eilat, too, has its beaches, the main one being on the North Shore. Further south the beaches are wider, the sand is whiter, and snorkeling in the coral reef, for which the Red Sea is

famous, is the main sport. Snorkeling lessons are available, and glass-bottomed boats and a submarine glide the less adventurous above and through the magical underwater coral world.

chapter seven

TRAVEL, HEALTH, & SECURITY

FLYING

Israel's international gateway, Ben Gurion Airport, inaugurated a new state-of-the-art Terminal 3 in 2005. Most visitors and Israelis are impressed by the sparkling new facility, its glossy departure hall with cascading ceiling-to-floor waterfall, cafés, and upmarket duty-free shops. Others resent the extra walking distances and miss the cozy ambience of the old arrangement.

Domestic flights use Terminals 1 and 2 at Ben Gurion and the Sde Dov airport just north of Tel Aviv. There are daily flights to Eilat and to Rosh Pina in the Galilee. Planes are packed with tourists, businessmen, and vacationing locals.

TAXIS

On exiting Ben Gurion, signs direct you to the taxi stands for various destinations where taxi coordinators fix the fare and order the cab. Otherwise cabs are flagged down or ordered by phone. Fares are either by the meter or agreed on in advance, according to an intercity table of fares set by the Ministry of Transport. There are surcharges at night, on Saturdays, and on public holidays, and for luggage. On prefixed cab fares a small tip may be expected, but is not obligatory. Generally, tipping is not expected.

Sherutim (singular, *sherut*) are shared taxis, mostly eight-seater minibuses that ply the busy city thoroughfares and intercity highways. In the city, passengers flag them down along the route. The intercity minibuses generally wait until all seats are taken before they depart. Fares are a little higher than regular bus fares.

BUSES

Israel's two main bus companies, Egged and Dan, supply most of the country's transportation needs. Both are cooperatives. Egged, the largest company by far, reaches the remotest parts of the country. Dan caters to the Greater Tel Aviv area. Buses are air-conditioned, clean, comfortable, well-maintained, and inexpensive. The drivers are courteous, helpful, and security trained. There are no conductors. You pay as you embark.

TRAINS

Israel Railways operates routes from Beersheva in the south to Nahariya in the north (one cannot reach Eilat by train). Trains are relatively inexpensive, modern, clean, punctual, and comfortable. Express trains run between the new international terminal at Ben Gurion Airport and Haifa and Jerusalem.

DRIVING

Road Traffic and Manners

In Israel you drive on the right-hand side of the road, and at intersections the vehicle entering from the left has the right of way. Highways are well maintained, but there aren't enough overpasses—in the morning and late afternoon entrances to the city and industrial areas can be

hopelessly congested. It's largely a matter of luck. Sometimes you get a clear run and at other times are stuck for ages. So if you have an appointment to keep, make an early start.

Auxiliary roads can be narrow and winding, particularly in the Galilee and Judean hills. Signs, especially for the visitor, can be confusing, forcing the driver to make fast and possibly risky decisions. Israel has suffered more fatalities from road accidents than from all its wars and terror attacks put together.

As in most countries, there are drivers who are aggressive and impatient, exceed the speed limit, weave suddenly in and out of traffic lanes, refuse to give way, drive too close to the car in front, and honk. There are bus and truck drivers who may fail to take into consideration the lethal nature of their vehicles. There are pedestrians who look neither to the left nor to the right when crossing the street. But, if there are drivers and pedestrians like this throughout the world, in Israel there are many more, particularly in the summers, which are hot and humid. There are many older vehicles that are not air-conditioned, and the patience of their drivers is tried to the limit.

Many Israelis, among them immigrants from North Africa and refugees from Europe, have learned to drive relatively late in life, when inexperience combined with diminished reflexes generally results in bad driving. There is a low level of vehicle maintenance because of its cost.

So do rent an air-conditioned car, and follow the rules. Keep a safe distance from other vehicles, and plan your route carefully before setting out. Take a map! And, of course, don't drink and drive. The legal blood alcohol level is 0.5 mg/ml.

Road Signs

Israel generally uses all the international road signs, and these are self-explanatory. Directions to major and tourist destinations are in Hebrew, Arabic, and English. Others may be in Hebrew only.

There is a dearth of signs warning the driver which lane to choose if he needs to leave the highway. A sign may come too late for the driver to do anything about it.

There can be confusion between speed limit and route signs. The number 60, for example, might be taken to mean either a sixty-kilometers-an-hour speed limit, or Route 60. This is avoided if you know that the two signs are shaped differently, the former a circle and the latter a rectangle.

Note that municipal signs may spell the name of their city one way, and national signs another. Drive from Tel Aviv toward the town of Herzliya, for example, and the first sign you'll see will spell it "Herzliyya;" the second, "Herzlia." There are alternative spellings for Caesarea (Qesariyya), Petach Tikvah (Petah Tiqva), and many other places. Initials are often used for towns, cities, and important streets—T. A. for Tel Aviv, P. T. for Petach Tikvah. The sign for Keren Kayemmet L'Israel Boulevard simply states " KKL Blvd."

SEEING THE COUNTRY

If you don't want to drive yourself, you can travel all over Israel by public transportation, by private car with an English-speaking driver guide, or by taking one of the many regular coach tours. The following brief descriptions highlight just a few of the many visitor attractions. The major cities and other towns offer a range of accommodation from cheap rooms up to five-star hotels; the rest up to three-and four-star accommodation.

Jerusalem

Less humid than the cities of the coastal plain, Jerusalem has clean mountain air and clear light. Here honey-colored limestone competes with glass and steel. Tall office buildings, hotels, and apartments rise above the narrow lanes and small squares of the old neighborhoods and the leafy, tree-lined streets of the new. Synagogues, mosques, and churches abut restaurants, cinemas, theaters, and shopping malls. Ancient wells, tunnels, and holy sites are minutes from soccer and basketball stadiums, parking lots, and gas stations. In summer, day and night, crowds throng the outdoor cafés.

Visit the Old City for its legendary Jewish, Christian, and Muslim holy sites—the Western Wall, the Mount of Olives, the Tomb of the Virgin, the Church of the Holy Sepulcher, the

Dome of the Rock, the al-Aqsa mosque, and many others. Pilgrims follow Christ's footsteps along the Via Dolorosa. Walk along the ramparts and see all the way to the Dead Sea, and linger in the markets and ancient lanes of the Muslim, Christian, Armenian, and Jewish quarters.

In West Jerusalem you can have a cup of coffee at the Knesset coffee shop and visit the nearby Israel Museum, with its permanent and current exhibitions, the Billy Rose sculpture garden, and the structure housing the Dead Sea Scrolls. Close by is the Givat Ram campus of the Hebrew University. You can attend a concert at the Sultan's Pool in the Hinnom Valley, and view the Chagall murals in the synagogue of the modern Hadassah Hospital. Stroll along the Haas/Sherover promenade for a breathtaking view of the Old City.

Jerusalem is a city of remembrance. The sacred Western Wall is a part of the supporting wall of Herod's Second Temple. (You can make a wish by leaving a note tucked into the cracks.) The Yad Vashem Museum commemorates the six and a half million who perished in the Holocaust. Also a city of profound and passionate beliefs, Jerusalem is most of all a place for prayer and contemplation, for reflection and discovery.

With more time to spend, venture further afield. You might visit Yemin Moshe, the nineteenth-century residential quarter built opposite the walls of the Old City, and today home to many local poets, writers, and artists. Ein Kerem, the birthplace of John the Baptist, is a charming village nestling in the valley below the Hadassah Medical Center, shaded by cypress and olive trees and dotted with churches, convents, and art galleries. Abu Ghosh is a Christian Arab town west of Jerusalem in the Judean  hills. It is crowned with a Romanesque church, dating back to Crusader times and famous for its acoustics, where regular concerts take place. Good Arab restaurants and lovely views attract both Jerusalemites and Tel Avivians.

Jerusalemites on the whole lack the spontaneity and *joie de vivre* of their Tel Aviv counterparts, and are more modest both in their dress and in their approach to life.

Tel Aviv–Jaffa

Tel Aviv is sometimes called the "White City," a legacy from the the Bauhaus School of Architecture that flourished during the 1920s and '30s, when leading German architects of the school immigrated to Israel. Their buildings, with plain white stucco exteriors, rounded balconies, and

windowed stairwells, bequeathed to Tel Aviv one of the largest concentrations of Bauhaus buildings in the world, and was declared a "World Heritage Site" by UNESCO in 1995. Over the years the buildings fell into a state of grayish peel, but today they are protected and are being restored. For a concentration of Bauhaus splendor, visit Lev Tel Aviv,

the "heart" of Tel Aviv, including Montefiori, Rothschild Boulevard, and Ahad Haam.

Other architectural influences came from Le Corbusier, and the need to provide housing for the rapid growth in population. The ugly rows of uniform, rectangular, shuttered, economy built, three- and four-story workers' apartment blocks called *shikunim* are today mostly concealed by trees and high hedges.

Tel Aviv–Jaffa is a city of tall green trees, shady boulevards, beaches, parks—the largest of which, the Yarkon Park, is situated on both sides of the Yarkon River—lively streets, bustling markets, and gleaming modern office and residential towers.

Stop in gentrified Neve Tzedek, Tel Aviv's oldest Jewish neighborhood. Stroll down Shabazi Street, lined with chic boutiques, arts and crafts shops, small restaurants, and cafés; explore the narrow lanes and courtyards; visit the Nachum Gutman Museum and the Suzanne Dellal Dance Center. The lively beachfront promenade passes a marina and imposing international and local hotels, and leads to the lanes and alleyways of Old Jaffa.

In Old Jaffa, visit the restored Turkish Quarter, and the picturesque artists' quarter, with its Crusader walls, cobbled streets, and ancient harbor. The architect-turned-sculptor Frank Meisler exhibits *objets d'art* made of gold, silver, and pewter. Enjoy sunset views from the terrace of the unusual Illana Goor Museum, Horrace Richter's Gallery, or the café-pub Alladin, and search for bargains in the flea market.

With an hour or so to spare, you can enjoy a walk on the promenade along the long white beach, stopping for coffee at one of the cafés along the way. Tel Aviv is a tolerant and a safe place. Women can and do walk alone at night almost anywhere and at any hour.

In Tel Aviv you can dine at many restaurants until the early morning, and lunch hours are flexible. One seaside restaurant serves its famous champagne breakfast till five in the afternoon. Cafés are open till late and pubs and wine bars close when the last guest leaves. Clubs, straight and gay, only open late and the city has its share of all-night red-light amenities. Fashionable streets, the Tel Aviv promenade, and outdoor cafés are crowded until after midnight, and in summer the beaches are never empty, with young Tel Avivians and backpacking tourists huddling around bonfires picnicking, singing, and playing guitars. Then at sunrise, as the last revelers go home to bed, the retirees do their early morning exercises.

Mediterranean in character, Tel Avivians are generally warm, friendly, spontaneous, and eager to live life to the full. They can also be quite inconsiderate, particularly when driving or talking on their cell phones.

Haifa

Haifa's residents are, by and large, a solid crew, holding sound secular values and not attracted to extremes—historically moderate Laborites who, over their morning cup of coffee, would first look at the view and then the morning's headlines.

A modern port city with theaters, museums, cinemas, hotels, shopping malls, and sandy beaches, Haifa owes its beauty to its setting. Hugging the slopes and spread out on the crest of Mount Carmel, it provides spectacular views in all directions. To the west, the Mediterranean, the ships in the bay; to the north, on a clear day, the coastline, including the ancient walled city of Acre, up to the Lebanese border; and to the southeast, the fertile, green Jezreel Valley.

Haifa has three levels, each with its own personality. The dockside area, like any other port, has small restaurants, pubs, and sleaze. The area is also home to Bat Galim, an attractive seafront residential and tourist neighborhood. The middle section, Hadar Hacarmel, is commercial and cultural, and is home to the Technion, the Israel Institute of Technology. The top section, the Carmel, is mainly residential and includes hotels, shopping areas, and Haifa University, a tall structure that can be seen from virtually anywhere

in the northwest of Israel. On the summit are forest nature reserves, with walking and cycling tracks, and panoramic views.

Drive along the Panorama Road for a dizzying view of the sea, lower city, port, and bay. Visit the Baha'i Temple and Gardens (book a tour in advance, as a limited number of tourists are allowed in daily). Have a snack or fish lunch at one of the restaurants on the new seaside promenade, or Middle Eastern specialties in the nearby Druze village of Daliat-El-Carmel on the summit of Mount Carmel.

Eilat

At this modern Red Sea resort you can watch the sun rise over the purple mountains and aquamarine waters of the Gulf of Aqaba, where you can swim, sunbathe even in the winter, and snorkel. Eilat is hot in summer and warm in winter, with great beaches, corals, deep-sea diving, entertainment facilities, and a unique underwater marine-life observation chamber.

Acre (Akko)

North of Haifa, this walled Crusader city (visit the Knights' Hall) is populated mainly by Arabs; there are adjacent Jewish neighborhoods. It is picturesque, with a busy bazaar and spice market, fish restaurants, and an old fishing harbor.

Nahariya

Israel's most northern city, established by German immigrants in the mid-1930s, has retained its German character. It is close to the steep, white cliffs of Rosh Hanikra on the Lebanese border, where a cable car takes tourists down to rocks and grottoes. With its stream flowing down the main street, horse-drawn carriages, and broad beach, it is a favorite with honeymooners.

Nazareth

Overlooking the Valley of Jezreel, half Arab Muslim and half Arab Christian, Nazareth is famous as the town where Jesus grew up. In addition to its religious buildings—more than forty churches, including the Basilica of the Annunciation, convents, monasteries, and mosques—there is a lively market.

Safed

This mystical hilltop town in Galilee has medieval streets and an artists' quarter, and is a center for ultra-Orthodox Jewish religious and philosophical studies. For escaping the heat, it's a popular summer resort among older Israelis.

Tiberias

On the Sea of Galilee, 700 feet (213 meters) below sea level, Tiberias was once a center of Jewish learning. It dates back to 18 CE, and has Crusader ruins, beaches, and an active waterfront. The city is rich in biblical lore and is an excellent base for exploring the Galilee and Golan Heights.

From the waterfront promenade there are

views across the lake—to the east, the Golan Heights, and to the northeast, on a clear day, the snowy peaks of Mount Hermon. You can have a spa treatment at the hot springs on the lakeshore, or a short distance away at Hammat Gader. Visit Capernaum (Kfar Nahum) and other biblical sites where Jesus preached and performed miracles; the Hula Nature Reserve, teeming with wildlife; and Rosh Pina, a charming hillside town with a restored old quarter. The nearby Kibbutz Ein Gev holds an annual music festival.

Caesarea

Named after Augustus Caesar, Caesarea was Herod's showpiece port city and the headquarters of Roman administration in Israel. The restored Roman amphitheater seats five thousand people, and operas, concerts, and dance are performed there in the summer against the backdrop of sea and skies. Explore the remains of the Crusader city and the Roman aqueduct. Visit the golf club for a round of golf, a drink, or lunch.

The Dead Sea and Masada

Part of the Great Rift Valley, 1,338 feet (408 meters) below sea level, the Dead Sea is the lowest point on earth. Visitors come for the curative powers of the sea, mud, and air, and the views are spectacular. Float (you can't sink!) in the thick, mineral-rich waters, indulge in a treatment at one of the spas, and try a mud bath.

Visit Herod's dramatic rock fortress at Masada, 1,300 feet (396 meters) above the shore. There is a cable car, but the athletic still prefer to climb, especially to see the sun rise over the sea.

HEALTH CARE AND EMERGENCY SERVICES

Israel enjoys a high standard of medical care, with health professionals trained to Western standards. There is an extensive network of general and specialized modern hospitals and health centers throughout the country. The National Health Insurance law of 1995 provides all Israeli residents with a standardized range of medical services, including hospitalization.

The Magen David Adom (Red Shield of David), which is Israel's equivalent of the Red Cross, provides emergency care and other services. Yad Sara is a volunteer service that lends medical equipment of all kinds to those who need it. It is customary for those who use the service, and can do so, to make a donation, in order to maintain it for those who can't.

There is also a high level of private medicine available, and those with private medical insurance can be treated by leading specialists in luxurious medical centers throughout the county.

A visitor to Israel needs no vaccination or immunization and can feel as safe in Israel as in any Western country.

Health Tips

Protect yourself from the sun and drink plenty of water. Tap water is safe, but most Israelis, if they can afford it, prefer mineral water, which is sold in large or small bottles. Although it is generally safe to eat street food, avoid unfamiliar spicy foods if you are sensitive. Most hotels have doctors on call.

Mosquitoes can be a problem on the coastal plain; there are plenty of repellent lotions or devices and antihistamines on the market.

If you cut yourself badly or are bitten by a dog (unlikely), get yourself to a hospital or first aid station for an anti-Tetanus injection.

Take normal precautions against AIDS.

Hospital emergency rooms and first aid stations provide emergency services to all those requiring them.

SAFETY AND SECURITY

The chances that a visitor will be caught up in an act of terrorism in Israel are slight. Normal, busy life goes on. But the rule, as in many other countries, is to play it safe.

Don't ignore unattended bags or parcels in public places. Report them immediately to the authorities or security personnel. Keep your own belongings with you.

Don't carry unauthorized firearms or other weapons about your person. Cooperate with security personnel who search your bags and scan your body at entrances to shopping malls, cinemas, hotels, restaurants, and other places.

Be patient if you find the road you are traveling on is temporarily closed while police sappers detonate a suspect unidentified object.

Draw the attention of police or security personnel to anyone you suspect because of their behavior or attire.

Obey instructions from police, bus drivers, and security personnel promptly and without question. Be vigilant on roads close to borders, and even more so across the Green Line, where it is inadvisable to drive after dark. Don't pick up hitchhikers, even those in army uniform.

Follow the lead of Israelis, and seek advice from them on where to go and what not to do.

chapter eight

BUSINESS BRIEFING

BUSINESS CULTURE
Changing Attitudes

In the early socialist years of the State, business was a dirty word. Israelis were expected to build, farm, and manufacture, to provide housing, food, and essential products. Buying and selling, brokerage, making profits, and earning commissions were viewed with disdain. Real estate agents were regarded as parasites. There was a tax on travel, and with the advent of television in Israel color was wiped off all programs before transmission, so that there wouldn't be some people with color TV and others without.

As time passed attitudes changed. With successive right-wing governments, the privatization of many government industries and services (today even kibbutzim are talking about privatization), the ambition and resourcefulness of the Israelis, and the impact of globalization, Israel became part of the wider world.

Some useful Israeli business Web sites are given at the back of the book.

Business Dress

There is a strong awareness of dress in Israeli business circles, and to make a good first impression you should tend toward the formal to show seriousness of intent and respect for your host. Later on, take your cue from your host. Female visitors should dress modestly, whether the host is religious or not. A revealing outfit could be misinterpreted.

As everywhere, dress codes in Israel are determined by occupation. In Israel, bankers, lawyers, accountants, real estate developers, and senior hoteliers are at the top end of formality, wearing suits and ties even in summer. Industrialists and those employed in the service industry are less formal. Real informality is most likely to be found in the high-tech industries.

Israelis notice a lack of color coordination, and especially the state of people's shoes. It wasn't so long ago that Israelis wore sandals to their business meetings—but you should wear good shoes in perfect condition.

PROTOCOL AND PRESENTATIONS

Because Israelis come from so many backgrounds it is difficult to predict their business styles in advance. However, most of the businesspeople you are likely to meet will conduct themselves in a British or American manner. Israelis are avid learners. They will have been on business trips themselves and will have picked up all the tips on the right way to behave.

Business Cards

Israeli businessmen tend to have bilingual business cards, or separate cards in Hebrew and in English (or another language, depending on the country with which they are doing business). For the visiting businessman an English-language card will suffice.

Meetings

Unless the visitor and his Israeli host speak some other common language, negotiations will be carried out in English. Presentations will be made in English and contracts drawn up in English, or in Hebrew with certified English translations. All state-of-the-art audio-visual presentation technology is available in Israel.

Israelis tend to be more physical than their overseas counterparts. An Israeli host may very well sit next to his guest rather than on his own side of the desk. Israelis are often unaware of intruding on someone else's space. They are, however, poor at introductions, so if there are people present in the meeting to whom you haven't been introduced it is perfectly acceptable to offer your hand, say, "*Shalom*," and introduce yourself.

PERSONAL RELATIONS

Israelis believe in the importance of establishing good personal relations in a business context, so there is every chance that they will invite the visiting guest for dinner, either at their homes or at a restaurant. Everything we have learned about gift giving, religious and secular attitudes, and manners naturally applies here as well.

Noncontroversial topics of conversation such as movies, books, travel, and sports, particularly soccer, are appropriate. Refrain from criticizing anything to do with Israel, even if your host himself does so. Don't even concur. Be noncommittal, and if possible change the subject.

If your host is an Arab Muslim you may be expected to take off your shoes before entering his home. Follow his lead. Also remember that Muslims consider the left hand unclean, so use your right hand for eating, for instance when scooping hummus from a communal plate with pita bread, even if you are left-handed. It is customary to leave a little food in front of you at the end of a meal to show the host that his fare was most satisfying.

NEGOTIATING STYLES

There are too many Israeli negotiating styles to enable one to generalize, depending as they do on the nature of the transaction, the age, level of experience, education, and background of the negotiator, the size and prestige of the business he represents, and his status in it. There are, nevertheless, elements that are common to all.

The fact that Israelis value good personal relations in their business dealings is a manifestation of their openness and directness and of the wish to make a good impression. They understand the long-term benefits of establishing trust and rapport. They are also great risk takers, even when entering into and maintaining business relationships.

Whether or not the Israeli negotiator is anxious to conclude the deal, he will be gracious and polite, although his concept of politeness may not always coincide with that of the foreign visitor. His basic survival instincts may lead him to use tactics that can seem rather over-assertive, to give himself the upper hand.

Whether or not he takes outside calls during a meeting, invites his guest out for lunch or home for dinner, or offers help of a general nature, will depend on the above factors. But even if the most uncompromising or brash Israeli departs from the basic norms of polite behavior, it will be unwittingly.

CONTRACTS AND FULFILLMENT

Although the English Law of Contracts applies in Israel, with modifications, Israelis tend to regard verbal commitments, including binding verbal agreements, with less seriousness than written contracts. Certain transactions in Israel must be in writing, for example, the purchase and sale of land and fixed property. The exception to this attitude is the diamond industry, where the traditional handshake is still held sacred.

One of the reasons for this distrust of verbal agreements is the common experience that unknowns, such as taxes and bureaucratic surprises, can change the nature of the deal and become an impediment to its fulfillment.

In addition, the courts in Israel are overburdened and cases can take a long time to be heard, so unless there is written evidence supporting the claim, the prospects of success are slim. Many disputes, including those involving substantial claims, are resolved through arbitration. There are also the Small Claims courts where the procedure is less formal and the process is quicker and simpler.

In general it can be said that Israeli businessmen act in good faith, have no hidden agendas, and have every intention of complying with their contractual obligations. If there are obstacles *en route* Israeli businessmen tend to believe that personal relations will help to overcome them.

WOMEN IN BUSINESS

Although the number of women in the Israeli workplace is large, very few women pursue dedicated careers. Many of those who do, however, reach high positions in business and the professions. One of the wealthiest heiresses in the world, an Israeli woman, watches over her holdings in Israel with style and acumen. An Israeli woman has built a cosmetics empire, and another an international swimwear fashion house. Others are leaders in fashion, food production, insurance, banking, and in the arts and entertainment.

If a visiting businessman finds that his Israeli counterpart is a woman, the relationship should be kept on a strictly professional level—although common courtesies such as opening the door for her would in most circumstances be appreciated. Israeli businesswomen have not discarded their femininity.

chapter nine

COMMUNICATING

LANGUAGE

Hebrew is an ancient Semitic language. The original language of the Old Testament, it continued to be used by Jews throughout the centuries for literary and liturgical purposes. In the Middle Ages different pronunciations grew up among Ashkenazim (*Ashkenaz* being the medieval Hebrew word for Germany) and Sephardim (*Sepharad* being the word for Spain).

וַיְדַבֵּר יְהֹוָה אֶל מֹשֶׁה לֵאמֹר דַּבֵּר אֶל אַהֲרֹן וְאֶל בָּנָיו
לֵאמֹר כֹּה תְבָרְכוּ אֶת בְּנֵי יִשְׂרָאֵל אָמוֹר לָהֶם
יְבָרֶכְךָ יְהֹוָה וְיִשְׁמְרֶךָ יָאֵר יְהֹוָה פָּנָיו אֵלֶיךָ
וִיחֻנֶּךָּ יִשָּׂא יְהֹוָה פָּנָיו אֵלֶיךָ וְיָשֵׂם לְךָ שָׁלוֹם
וְשָׂמוּ אֶת שְׁמִי עַל בְּנֵי יִשְׂרָאֵל וַאֲנִי אֲבָרֲכֵם

In the late nineteenth century Hebrew was revived as a secular language by the Haskalah ("enlightenment") movement in Europe, and with the rise of Zionism it was adopted as the official language of the State of Israel, where it is spoken with a modified Sephardic accent.

The Hebrew alphabet is written from right to left, and for general purposes uses only consonants (vowel pointing exists, but is understood). Visitors need not worry, as most important signs and notices are written in English characters, or in English, as well, as are menus in many restaurants.

The second official language is Arabic. Hebrew is the most widely spoken, but Arabic is used in Arab schools, in Muslim religious courts, and in intercity directional signage. Arabic is taught in Israeli schools as a literary rather than a spoken language, and after school is soon forgotten.

English is widely spoken, as it is well taught in schools. At higher levels of business, in the professions, academe, and government, it is almost universally understood. The Russian immigration of the 1990s has established Russian as an important language, often used in commerce.

More than 50 percent of the Jews in Israel are Israeli-born, but their parents or grandparents came from more than a hundred different countries and spoke about eighty-five different languages or major dialects. One can still hear German, Yiddish, French, Spanish, Polish, Romanian, Hungarian, and others—languages from all the countries in which Jews resided before their immigration to Israel, including Amharic, which is spoken in Ethiopia. There are twelve different language broadcasts.

ELIEZER BEN YEHUDA

Hebrew was transformed in the late nineteenth century by a scholar from Lithuania, Eliezer Ben Yehuda (1858–1922), who settled in Israel in 1881. He refused to speak any other language and dedicated himself to the revival of Hebrew as a living tongue, able to meet modern needs. His most outstanding contribution was the dictionary of "Ancient and Modern Hebrew." He also founded the Hebrew Language Council to promote, regulate, and develop the Hebrew language.

Visitors quickly learn the Hebrew word *shalom*, which means "peace," and is used for both "hello" and "good-bye." Other words a visitor will soon pick up are: *hutzpah* (what a cheek!); *dafka* (in spite of); *bevakashah* (please); *todah* (thank you); *beseder* (okay); *betah* (of course); *bidiyuk* (exactly); *ken* (yes); *lo* (no); *boker tov* (good morning); *erev tov* (good evening); *laila tov* (good night); *ma shlomcha?* (how are you, to a male); *ma shlomaych?* (how are you, to a female); *slicha* (excuse me); *kama ze oleh?* (how much does it cost); *balagan* (mess, actually a Russian word); and *mazal tov* (congratulations).

Lost in Translation

The writer, soon after his immigration to Israel, and after studying Hebrew at an ulpan, was looking for an address. He'd been told to turn left after the first traffic lights (*ramzorim*), and after driving for some time and not finding the traffic lights in question, he stopped to seek help from some pedestrians. In his brand-new Hebrew he asked, "Where are the *mamserim* [bastards]?" "Bastards?" was the reply, "Which bastards do you want? We have more than enough around here."

BODY LANGUAGE

Talking with one's hands, arm waving, handshaking, hugging, kissing, back patting, arm touching, triumphant and obscene gesticulating (you'll know which is which), standing or sitting too close, squeezing, shrugging (Israeli kids learn to shrug at an early age), are all part of the wide lexicon of Israeli nonverbal communications. Israelis adopt few defensive postures.

THE MEDIA

Television

Israel has three state-managed channels: Channel One and Channel Thirty-Three, which operate under the IBA (the Israel Broadcast Authority), and Israel Educational TV, which operates as a unit of the Ministry of Education. The latter is screened on Channel Twenty-Three, with additional broadcasts on Channel One and Channel Two. There are also four public commercial channels, Two and Ten (Hebrew), Twenty-Four (Arabic), and Nine (Russian).

Hour-long Hebrew-language news programs are broadcast every evening on Channel One at 9:00 p.m., and on Channels Two and Ten at 8:00 p.m. All three channels broadcast the news headlines every half hour from 6:45 till 10:00 a.m. in the morning, and Channel Ten features a special fifteen-minute children's news broadcast at 7:30 a.m. daily. There is a daily English-language news broadcast on Channel One.

All the channels air sitcoms, soap operas, and movies, imported and local, current affairs, sports (including live coverage of soccer, basketball, and other games), news commentaries, politics, music, cooking, travel, fashion, features on cultural and social issues, programs for children, programs for new immigrants, and a host of others. The three state-managed channels include Arabic-language programs in their daily broadcasts, mostly tailored to the interests of the Arab community

Popular talk-show topics include religion, lifestyles, gender and cultural issues, and, first and foremost, politics. Some of these programs, particularly those on politics, end in chaos, with the participants interrupting each other and the host, and all talking at the same time.

Cable and satellite channels and multiple-channel providers include CNN, BBC World, and Sky News, plus entertainment programs in a host of languages.

Radio

Various radio channels offer news on the hour, local news in English and other languages, current affairs, sports, including live coverage, twenty-four-hour news coverage, traffic reports, and music, both popular (Israeli, mainstream, and Middle Eastern) and classical. The BBC World Service is popular among the older generation of English-speaking Israelis.

Details of English-language television and radio broadcasts may be found in the English-language newspapers.

The Press

A free press is a key component of Israel's democracy, and nothing is held sacred. Seven Hebrew-language papers are published daily, plus an additional eleven in other languages, including two in English. The four leading Hebrew-language dailies are *Yedioth Ahronoth*, *Maariv*, *Ha'aretz*, and *Globes*, Israel's equivalent of the *Financial Times*. The two English-language daily papers are the veteran *Jerusalem Post* and the English version of *Ha'aretz*, which is delivered together with the same day's *International Herald Tribune*. The leading national dailies of the U.S.A., U.K., Germany, France, Italy, and other Western countries are also available in Israel on the day of publication, or the day after.

There are numerous glossy Hebrew-language magazines featuring lifestyle, fashion, cuisine, travel, economics, army, Internet, sports, computers, motor vehicles, and entertainment. There are Russian-language magazines, and for English speakers, in addition to the wide choice of international magazines, there are the weekly *Jerusalem Post* and *Ha'aretz* lifestyle magazines, *The Jerusalem Report*, and the magazines published by the English-speaking residents' associations.

All the large Hebrew dailies are published on the Internet, as are numerous magazines catering to special interests. *Globes* also has an English-language Internet version.

TELEPHONE

Owned and operated by a government ministry until 1985, Israel's telephone network was pathetically unable to meet the country's needs. By 1980 the waiting list for telephone lines had reached 208,000. Local and international calls were outrageously expensive, and the time it took to install a new line or repair an existing line was excessively long.

In 1985 a state-controlled telecommunications company, Bezek, took over responsibility for the network, and in 1991 the company was floated on the Tel Aviv Stock Exchange, with the government selling 13.8 percent of its shares. During the 1990s, private-sector companies were permitted to enter the cell phone and international calling services market. The competition led to vastly improved communication services and lowered cell phone and overseas tariffs to among the lowest in the world. The waiting list for telephone lines is a thing of the past, and there are many innovative services being developed in Israel.

The official telephone directory is the *Yellow Pages*, a combination of subscriber telephone numbers and advertisements printed in Hebrew, with English versions for different postal areas. One can dial 144 for directory information.

The cellular phone market is served by four companies. In mid 2000 the number of cellular phones surpassed the number of landlines, with some 66 percent of the population owning a cell phone, one of the highest per capita in the world.

Cell phone numbers are freely given out, and Israelis will answer calls at all times.

A successful television ad with the slogan "Israelis love to talk to each other" showed a group of friends standing side by side on a balcony each engrossed in their own cell phone conversation.

MAIL

In 1987 the Postal Authority took over responsibility for mail from the Communications Ministry. Over the next ten years the postal services improved, with the number of items delivered in Israel and abroad increasing by 70 percent, cutting delivery time from five to one or two days, and the establishment of messenger and security courier services. The number of annual express-mail items grew from 20,000 in 1987 to more than three million at the turn of the century.

But beware. If a mailed item is too large for the home mailbox it will be returned to the post office, from where it must be collected. Two reminders will be sent, and if the item is not collected within a certain time it will be returned to the sender. On the other hand, postal clerks, once abrupt and unhelpful, now live up to the image of the smart red-and-white post offices and their service is generally friendly and professional. Their customers now wait patiently for attention in disciplined lines.

Postmen don't wear uniforms.

CONCLUSION

In this overview there has inevitably been a reliance on many generalizations, unavoidable when writing about a country as diverse as Israel, but the facts are remarkable. In less than sixty years Israel has grown from a strip of land containing little more than 600,000 Jewish inhabitants to a Jewish population numbering more than 5,000,000. A country of immigration, it has absorbed people from all corners of the globe, some in waves and others in trickles, many of whom, in the early years, were damaged in mind and body by their experiences under the Nazis, others from third-world countries, lacking in education and familiarity with modern institutions and mores.

From an agriculture-based, poor economy, Israel has developed industries, particularly in high technology, and innovative products and services that are world leaders in their fields. In the course of defending itself in wars and with continuing threats to its security, the Israel Defense Force has become a formidable fighting machine, while at the same time retaining its "citizens' army" ethos. Israel's infrastructure in almost all areas matches those of the most advanced of modern states. Its democratic institutions are among the most enlightened.

These facts alone might not be enough to persuade the reader to pack his or her bags for a visit, other than for business or some other specialized purpose. More compelling are the attractions of Israel's cities, its historical and religious landmarks, its rich cultural life, its countryside, its beaches, seas, and almost year-round sunshine, and, finally, its people. For along with the energy, courage, intelligence, and resourcefulness that in a brief span of history have produced so much change and progress, there is openness, spontaneity, and an irresistible passion for life, that makes every visit a pleasurable experience. Another generalization? Just try it!

Further Reading

Bar Zohar, Michael. *Ben Gurion.* New York: Delcorte, 1978.

Bellow, Saul. *To Jerusalem and Back.* New York: Secker & Warburg, 1976.

Elon, Amos. *The Israeli Founders and Sons.* London: Weidenfeld & Nicolson, 1971.

Geri, Jeffrey. *The Trouble with Francis.* U.S.: Xlibris, Israel Vertical Press, 2002.

Geri, Jeffrey. *Oh Henry.* U.S.: Xlibris, Israel Vertical Press, 2000.

Herzog, Haim. *The Arab–Israeli Wars.* New York: Random House, 1982.

Koestler, Arthur. *Thieves in the Night: Chronicle of an Experiment.* London: Macmillan, 1946.

Rosenthal, Donna. *The Israelis. Ordinary People in an Extraordinary Land.* New York: Free Press/Simon & Schuster, 2005

Rothenberg, Naftali. *Jewish Identity in Modern Israel.* Jerusalem: Urim Publications, 2002

Rubinstein, Amnon. *The Zionist Dream Revisited.* New York: Schocken Books, 1984.

Shimshoni, Daniel. *Israel Democracy.* New York: Free Press, 1982.

Soans, Robin. *The Arab–Israeli Cookbook.* London: Aurora Metro Press, 2004.

Yehoshua, A. B. *The Lover.* New York: Dutton, 1985.

In-Flight Hebrew. NewYork: Living Language, 2001.

Other Israeli authors include Amos Oz (Harcourt), David Grossman (Farrar, Strauss & Giraux), and Meir Shalev (Harper Collins).

Business Web Sites

Federation of Israeli Chambers of Commerce: www.chamber.org.il/english

Manufacturers Association of Israel: www.industry.org.il/eng

The Israeli Export and International Cooperation Institute: www.export.gov.il/eng/

Index

Acknowledgments

If it hadn't been for my wife Wendy's research, input, insight, and computer skills, this book would not have come to life. I thank her for her help and encouragement. For twenty-eight years Director of Public Relations at the Sheraton Tel Aviv Hotel and Towers, she, if anyone, knows what visitors to Israel want and expect.